TREES and SHRUBS of the ADIRONDACKS

William K. Chapman
and Alan E. Bessette

Published by
North Country Books, Inc.
Utica, New York

Copyright © 1990
by
William K. Chapman
and
Alan E. Bessette

ISBN 0-932052-75-4

All Rights Reserved

No part of this book may be reproduced in any manner without the written permission of the authors except for brief quotes for review purposes.

All photographs by William K. Chapman and Alan E. Bessette unless otherwise noted.

Neither the authors nor the publisher accept responsibility for identifications made by persons who use this book. In addition, they do not accept responsibility for any adverse effects which may arise from ingesting any part of these plants. Species known to be edible for many people may cause unpleasant reactions in others. They cannot predict individual reactions and cannot accept responsibility for experimentation.

Library of Congress Cataloging-in-Publication Data

Chapman, William K., 1951-
    Trees and shrubs of the Adirondacks / by William K. Chapman and Alan E. Bessette.
      p.   cm.
    Includes indexes.
    ISBN 0-932052-75-4 : $13.95
    1. Trees—New York (State)—Adirondack Park—Identification.
    2. Shrubs—New York (State)—Adirondack Park—Identification.
    3. Trees—New York (State)—Adirondack Park—Pictorial works.
    4. Shrubs—New York (State)—Adirondack Park—Pictorial works.
    I. Bessette, Alan.   II. Title.
QK177.C46   1989
582.1609747'53—dc 19   89-3219
                                                                                         CIP

North Country Books, Inc.
Utica, New York 13501

TABLE OF CONTENTS

Acknowledgments	5
Introduction	6
Arrangement of the Book	7
How to Use the Key	10
Key to the Trees and Shrubs	11
Descriptions — Section I: Cedar, Pine and Yew Families	15
Descriptions — Section II: The Broad-Leaved Families	23
Color Plates	50
Descriptions — Section II continued	85
How to Make a Pressed Leaf Collection	117
Glossary	118
Visual Glossary	122
Index to Common Names	126
Index to Botanical Names	129

LIST OF ILLUSTRATIONS

Paper Birch	Title Page
American Yew	15
Fire Cherry	23
Gray Birch	32
Cassandra	121
Canada Plum	38
Common Gooseberry	40
Sand Cherry	47
Blackberry Leaf	86
Raspberry Leaf	87
Highbush Blueberry	100
Basswood Fruit	107

ACKNOWLEDGMENTS

Several people have helped to make this field guide possible. We thank Valerie Conley for providing technical assistance. Diana Bessette and Vicki Haines read the manuscript, provided technical assistance, and made useful suggestions for improving the book. Ann and John Kapcio assisted us in collecting specimens and were especially generous by providing the use of their camp. We are grateful to Philippa Brown for providing several drawings distributed throughout the text. We thank Audrey Sherman for typesetting and for making valuable suggestions for improving the manuscript. We are also grateful to John Mahaffy for designing the book. We especially thank Sheila Orlin, Robert Igoe, and Arthur Dischiavo for their guidance and creativity, and for giving us the opportunity to write this book.

PHOTO CREDITS

John Kapcio provided the photographs of Juneberry (Plate 13, No. 1) and Pale Laurel (Plate 25, No. 2).

INTRODUCTION

This book is a field guide to the trees and shrubs found in the Adirondack area, but not restricted to it. Although the photographs were taken of trees and shrubs growing in the Adirondacks, many of the species are found throughout New York State and in many parts of New England.

The growing "back to nature" movement has sparked renewed interest in the environment and a curiosity about the plants and animals that share the world around us. Identifying trees and shrubs is becoming more popular in all parts of the country, especially the richly forested Adirondacks. Love of the outdoors, interest in natural history, general human curiosity, scientific interest, or whatever the reason, identifying trees and shrubs is a fascinating and enjoyable experience.

Our purpose in presenting this regional guide is to enable the non-botanist to identify the trees and shrubs found in the Adirondacks. Much of the technical language has been eliminated. A glossary, combined with simple keys and easy to follow descriptions, makes identifications fast and accurate.

Our primary task in approaching this work was to define the geographic area of the Adirondacks. For this book, we confined our study to the exact boundaries of the Adirondack Park as it is outlined on New York State maps. Concentration within these boundaries and exclusion of the surrounding foothills has been a major factor in shaping the final character of this work. Had we extended our area of study outward only ten additional miles, we would have been obliged to include the sycamore, black locust, redbud, spicebush, sassafras, and others. The box elder was the most marginal species. At one location it was found in sight of the park boundary marker, although we found no evidence of it within the park. Conversely, if the boundaries of the park shrank inwards by ten miles, this would have eliminated most of the oaks, an elm and possibly some hickories.

ARRANGEMENT OF THE BOOK

This guide contains 140 color photographs and corresponding descriptions. If no plate number is listed, then there is no corresponding photograph. Plate locations for similar species are found only in the indices. Photographs and descriptions have been arranged by families within two major categories—the conifer group and the broad-leaf group. Each photograph in this guide shows the major features used to identify the species. Each description lists the important characteristics used in the identification process. The plate numbers indicated beneath each photograph are listed on the corresponding descriptions.

The main criterion for differentiating trees and shrubs from herbaceous vegetation is that the stalk or trunk be both woody and perennial. In cases such as bristly sarsaparilla (*Aralia hispida*) this may apply only to the base of the main stalk.

The distinction between trees and shrubs is both artificial and arbitrary and serves man's convenience, not the plants. In the past, this distinction has been based either on height or the number of stalks arising from a single root. We have accepted the ability of an adult specimen to exceed 20 feet in height as the deciding factor in classifying a species as either a tree or a shrub. As it was our intention to focus primarily on the larger trees and shrubs, we have not included any woody plant normally under 12 inches in height. This has eliminated plants such as crowberries, dewberries, and the shorter heaths which include bearberry, bilberry and others. In addition, it has been our decision not to include woody vines such as grape or Virginia creeper in this survey.

Common name: A common name has been provided for each species included in this guide. Whenever more than one common name is available for a species, the regional preference is used. Although some species have multiple common names and more than one species can have the same common name, they are however, frequently used, and therefore included in this book.

Botanical name: The botanical name indicated for each species is unique—only one species will have this name. Application of the botanical name avoids confusion, and with a little practice, the somewhat intimidating Latin names become easier to use. In addition, when translated, the botanical name is often descriptive of the plant. It consists of two parts, a genus (first letter capitalized, remaining letters lower case) and species (all letters lower case). For example, *Acer saccharum (Acer* = maple, *saccharum* = sugar) describes a maple tree from which a sugary sap is obtained.

Family name: The family name for each species illustrated is listed both in its scientific and common forms. The family name indicates specific characteristics which all genera and species have in common. Identification of the family allows the reader to compare a particular species to others in the same group. All species within a family will share one or more major features.

Description: Information about size, overall shape, trunk and branch features, leaves, and bark is provided in this section. The descriptions have been based primarily on characteristics evident for long periods, such as leaves and bark. Additional characteristics such as flowers and fruits have also been included when appropriate. Measurements are given in English units becuase they are familiar to most people.

Each description begins with the size of the plant in question. The first measurement given is the normal size of that species within the Park. If that species grows to greater size in parts of its range outside the Park, then those figures are given in parentheses.

This section also lists the flowering and fruiting seasons for many trees and shrubs. This information is included to assist the reader who may wish to photograph the plants at these stages. Those dates given reflect the peak period during which 90% of that species should be in either flower or fruit. Minority populations that fall outside the main seasons have not been taken into account here because their inclusion would render this data impractical for use. An example of this is the blue elderberry. In this case, 5% of the specimens encountered may still bear ripe berries a full two months past the prime fruiting season.

Much of our fieldwork in this area was done from a camp at Piseco Lake. For this reason, the flowering and fruiting seasons given are those for the Piseco Lake region. It should be noted that through mid-summer the stated seasons will occur one to two weeks later in the northern Adirondack region. Plants living in areas of higher altitude than the Piseco region (about 2,500 feet above sea level) will also have later flowering and fruiting seasons.

Occurrence: This section contains information about where trees and shrubs grow. Some plants have very specialized habitats such as bogs, while others grow in a more generalized habitat. Many prefer dry, sandy soils while others prefer moist soil.

Similar species: Trees and shrubs which are closely related or those that morphologically resemble the illustrated species are briefly described in this section. Carefully compare your unknown specimen to the illustrated species, read the corresponding description, then read the information in this section before reaching a final decision.

If a tree or shrub listed under similar species does not have a separate listing elsewhere in the book (ex. *Ilex laevigata*), then it may be assumed that the species whose description is given above and in greater detail is the more common of the two. The only exceptions to this would be blueberries, willows, juneberries, raspberries, and blackberries. These groupings include closely related species so similar in appearance that giving each its own listing would become unnecessarily repetitive in terms of time and space.

Comments: This section includes a variety of information including diagnostic (key) features, synonyms, edibility, uses, origin of names, and other useful remarks.

HOW TO USE THE KEY

This key has been designed to help the reader determine the major group, family, or species to which a specimen belongs. As an alternative, one may thumb through the book until a photograph is found which matches the unknown specimen. This can often be an inefficient and frustrating approach to identification of trees and shrubs. Therefore, the use of the key is strongly recommended.

This key is primarily based on the leaf structure of trees and shrubs. Major groups and families share similar leaf features, making it easy to place an unknown specimen into its correct family. To identify a plant to species, it is sometimes also necessary to consider other features, such as flowers or fruit. In most instances, these features can easily be seen with the unaided eye. In a small number of cases, the use of a hand lens will prove useful.

To determine the species, always start at the beginning of the key. Read the information beside the Roman numerals I and II to decide whether your specimen is a member of the pine/yew family (I), or a member of the broad-leaved families (II). Underneath the appropriate heading, read the information provided beside A, B, C, D and E. This information will describe the type of leaf and its arrangement on the branch. If any of the terms used, such as palmate-compound or opposite, are unfamiliar to you, refer to the Glossary and Visual Glossary for assistance. Using this information, select the letter that describes the leaf characteristics of your specimen. Directly beneath this letter, you will find a final set of choices in the form of numbered descriptions of plant families or species. Choose the description that matches your plant, and then turn to the pages indicated and compare the specimen to the desciptions provided. To further assist in identification, compare the specimen to the corresponding photographs. Be sure to read the information presented under "Similar Species" in the event that the specimen is described there.

KEY TO THE TREES AND SHRUBS OF THE ADIRONDACKS

This key will assist the reader in identifying any unknown tree or shrub encountered within the Adirondack Park. The authors wish to point out that this key applies only to this area. Characteristics of certain plant families vary in different sections of the country. Because of this, the effectiveness of this key may be lessened if used outside the park boundaries.

I. The Cedar, Pine and Yew Families. Leaves usually needle-like and evergreen, except for *Larix laricina*. Fruit a woody cone, except for *Taxus canadensis*.
   A. Leaves flat, blade-like, ½-1¼ inches long.
      1. Leaves dark green above, pale green beneath, short-stalked. *Taxus canandensis*: Page 16.
      2. Leaves dark green above, paler with greenish white stripes beneath.
         a. Leaves not stalked. Cones erect, not persisting. *Abies balsamea*: Page 16.
         b. Leaves stalked. Cones pendant, persisting. *Tsuga canadensis*: Page 17.
   B. Leaves needle-like, growing in clusters.
      1. Needles in clusters of two.
         a. Needles ½-1½ inches long. *Pinus banksiana*: Page 17.
         b. Needles 1½-3 inches long. *Pinus sylvestris*: Page 19.
         c. Needles 4-7 inches long. *Pinus resinosa*: Page 18.
      2. Needles in clusters of three. *Pinus rigida*: Page 18.
      3. Needles in clusters of five. *Pinus strobus*: Page 19.
      4. Needles in clusters of eight or more. *Larix laricina*: Page 20.
   C. Leaves three-sided needles ¼-½ inch long; or leaves egg-shaped, small, and overlapping.
      1. Leaves egg-shaped, overlapping, ⅛ inch long. *Thuja occidentalis*: Page 20.
      2. Leaves on older growth egg-shaped, overlapping, ¹⁄₁₆

inch long. Leaves on new growth needle-like, ¼ inch long. *Juniperus virginiana*: Page 21.
3. Leaves needle-like, ⅓-½ inch long, in whorls of three around the twigs. *Juniperus communis* var. *depressa*: Page 21.

D. Leaves needle-shaped, short, up to 1 inch long, sharp, stiff, square in cross section, growing singly off the twigs.
  1. Twigs minutely hairy (use hand lens).
    a. Cones 1-2 inches long, oval, not persisting. *Picea rubens*: Page 22.
    b. Cones ¾-1¼ inch long, round, persistent. *Picea mariana*: Page 22.
  2. Twigs not minutely hairy.
    a. Cones ½-2½ inches long. *Picea glauca*: Page 22.
    b. Cones 4-7 inches long. *Picea abies*: Page 22.

II. The broad-leaved trees and shrubs. Leaves shed each fall, except for a few members of the heath family.
  A. Leaves simple, alternate.
    1. Leaves toothed. Flowers and fruit in catkins. Seeds tiny, downy, dispersed by wind. Willow family - *Salicaceae*: Pages 24-27.
    2. Leaves double-toothed, in some species asymmetrical. Fruit a small cone, cone-like, or a single nut or nutlet within a leaf-like bract. Birch family - *Betulaceae*: Pages 30-33.
    3. Leaves lobed or with large, even teeth. Flowers in catkins. Fruit an acorn, or a spined burr containing 2-3 nuts. Beech family - *Fagaceae*: Pages 34-37.
    4. Leaves coarsely toothed, asymmetrical. Flowers inconspicuous, greenish. Fruit flat circular keys or berry-like with a large seed. Elm family - *Ulmaceae*: Pages 38-39.
    5. Leaves broad, maple-like. Flowers in drooping clusters. Fruit a berry. Stems and fruit often spined or prickled. Gooseberry family - *Grossulariaceae*: Pages 40-41.
    6. Leaves toothed. Flowers with 5 usually white, some-

times pink, petals. Fruit variable, from fleshy to dry capsules. Rose family - *Rosaceae*: Pages 42-49, 85.
    7. Leaves toothless, evergreen in some species, sometimes downy on the underside. Flowers usually cylindrical to bell-shaped, with 5 lobes at the opening. Fruit highly variable, from juicy berries to dry capsules. Heath family - *Ericaceae*: Pages 95-96, 98-101.
    8. Leaves simple, alternate, but not fitting into the above families. Pages 110-114.

B. Leaves simple, opposite.
    1. Leaves broad, toothed, long-stemmed, with 3-5 lobes. Flowers small, in clusters. Fruit paired, long-winged keys. Maple family - *Aceraceae*: Pages 90-92.
    2. Leaf margins not toothed. Flowers 4-petaled, in showy terminal clusters. Fruit berry-like, single-seeded, in terminal clusters. Dogwood family - *Cornaceae*: Pages 93-95.
    3. Leaves opposite, or in whorls of three. Flowers bowl-shaped with 5 shallow lobes, pink or red, in clusters. Fruit a woody capsule. Heath family - *Ericaceae*: Page 97.
    4. Leaf margins either smooth or toothed. Flowers tubular, with 5-6 elongated lobes or 5 rounded petal-like lobes. Fruit variable, berry-like to woody capsules, single to several seeded. Honeysuckle family - *Caprifoliaceae*; Pages 102-104, 106-109.
    5. Leaves simple, opposite or whorled, but not fitting into the above families. Pages 114-115.

C. Leaves palmately compound, alternate.
    1. Stem angled, thorned. Fruit a berry. Rose family - *Rosaceae*: Page 86.

D. Leaves pinnately compound, alternate.
    1. Leaflets toothed. Flowers in catkins. Fruit a thick-shelled nut, enclosed in a husk which may or may not split into 4 sections at maturity. Walnut family - *Juglandaceae*: Pages 28-29.
    2. Leaflets toothed. Flowers with 5 petals, white or pink, solitary or clustered. Fruit orange to red to

black, shape variable, several seeded. Rose family - *Rosaceae*: Pages 87-89.
    3. Leaflets toothed. Flowers greenish, small. Flowers and red fruit in conspicuous upright conical clusters 8-12 inches tall. Cashew family - *Anacardiaceae*: Page 90.
    4. Leaves compound, alternate, but not fitting into the above families. Page 116.
E. Leaves pinnately compound, opposite.
    1. Leaflets smooth or toothed. Flowers small, in clusters. Fruit clusters of long-winged keys. Olive family - *Oleaceae*: Page 102.
    2. Leaflets toothed. Flowers small, cream or white, in large clusters. Fruit small berries, several seeded, in large clusters. Honeysuckle family - *Caprifoliaceae*: Page 105.
    3. Leaves compound, opposite, but not fitting into the above families. Page 115-116.

Section I

The Cedar, Pine and Yew Families

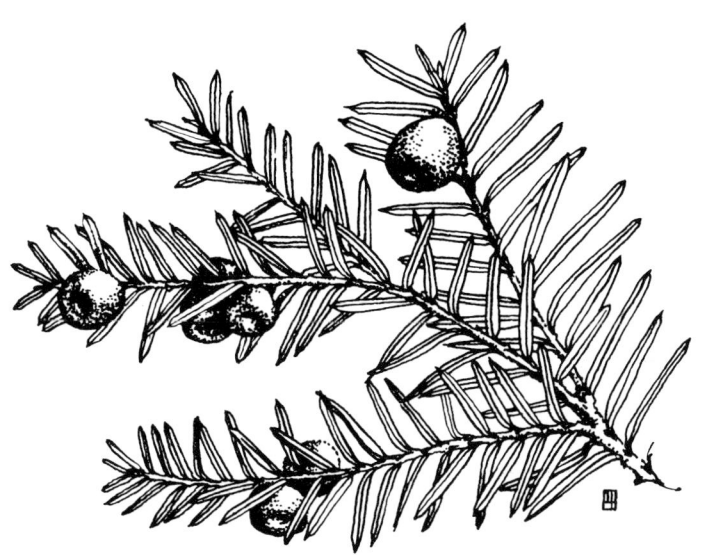

American Yew
Taxus canadensis, page 16

AMERICAN YEW   YEW FAMILY
Taxus canadensis   *Taxaceae*
Plate 1, No. 1

Description: Shrub 1-3 (occasionally 4 or more) feet tall, forming dense spreading clumps of branches. Leaves simple, borne flatly on opposite sides of the branchlets, ¾-1 inch long, blade-like, flat, abruptly pointed, short-stalked, dark green on the upper surface, slightly paler beneath, evergreen. Fruit ¼-½ inch in diameter, oval, consisting of a hard, brown, oval seed surrounded by a thick, soft, smooth, red, berry-like cup, ripening in late summer. Bark yellowish brown to dark brown, nearly smooth. *Occurrence*: Moist soil in conifer or mixed woods. *Similar species*: Thickets of young hemlock (*Tsuga canadensis*) closely resemble mature yew plants, but the needles of hemlock have two distinct white stripes on their underside. *Comments*: Also known as Canada yew and ground hemlock. The red, berry-like cup is edible, but all other parts of the plant contain a poisonous alkaloid called taxine. The Adirondacks' only known toxic conifer.

BALSAM FIR   PINE FAMILY
Abies balsamea   *Pinaceae*
Plate 1, No. 2

Description: Tree 20-60 (rarely 80) feet tall, trunk straight; branches horizontal. Leaves simple, borne flatly on opposite sides of the branchlets, ½-1¼ inches long, blade-like, flat, tips rounded or notched, dark blue-green above, paler with two white stripes beneath, evergreen. Cones 2-4 inches long, nearly oval, purple-brown when young, becoming pale brown in age, growing erect on the branches, not persisting; scales very thin, flat, broadly rounded; seeds paired, long-winged, resinous. Bark gray or brown, smooth, covered with raised blisters. *Occurrence*: From swampy ground to high mountain peaks. *Similar species*: Canadian hemlock (*Tsuga canadensis*) also has flat needles that are striped on the underside, but they are only about ½ inch long. *Comments*: Popular Christmas tree because of its aromatic odor and tendency to retain needles for extended periods. Reduced to a low spreading shrub under harsh conditions at higher elevations. The only native fir of the northeastern states.

EASTERN HEMLOCK PINE FAMILY
Tsuga canadensis *Pinaceae*
Plate 1, No. 3

Description: Tree 50-80 feet tall, trunk straight; branches horizontal, with drooping, feathery branchlets. Leaves simple, borne flatly on opposite sides of the branchlets, approximately ½ inch long, blade-like, flat, tips blunt or sometimes minutely notched, short-stalked, dark green on the upper surface, paler with two white stripes beneath, evergreen. Cones up to ¾ inch long, oval, grayish brown, hanging from the tips of the branchlets; scales few, thin, rounded; seeds winged. Bark brown or purple-brown, deeply furrowed. *Occurrence*: Common on low swampy ground, near streams, and on rocky slopes. *Similar species*: Norway spruce (*Picea abies*) has a similar profile, because of the drooping, plume-like branchlets. It may be quickly differentiated by its 4-sided needles and its 4-7 inch cones. *Comments*: Important source of lumber. The bark is used in the tanning of leather goods. The needles are the shortest and darkest of all Adirondack evergreens.

NORTHERN SCRUB PINE PINE FAMILY
Pinus banksiana *Pinaceae*
Plate 1, No. 4

Description: Tree 15-25 (occasionally 60 or more) feet tall, with wide spreading branches. When growing in rocky, exposed habitats, this species is often stunted, distorted, shrub-sized. Leaves ½-1½ inches long, simple, needle-shaped, sharp-pointed, rigid, twisted, dark green, in clusters of two which diverge at a wide angle, evergreen. Cones 1-2 inches long, cone-shaped, tip curved and pointed towards the branch tip, light yellow to dark brown, usually occurring in pairs, persisting; scales blunt, thickened at the tip, with a prickle when young, smooth when mature, often remaining closed and holding seeds for years. Bark dark brown to grayish, scaly. *Occurrence*: Barren, sandy or dry soil, usually in exposed habitats. *Similar species*: Red pine (*P. resinosa*) and scotch pine (*P. sylvestris*) also bear needles in clusters of two, but those of the red pine are 4-6 inches in length and those of the scotch pine are up to 3 inches long. *Comments*: Was *P. divaricata*.

RED PINE   PINE FAMILY
Pinus resinosa   *Pinaceae*
                                                                   Plate 2, No. 1

Description: Tree 50-80 (occasionally 100 or more) feet tall, trunk straight; branches irregular and spreading. Leaves 4-6 (occasionally 8) inches long, simple, slender, needle-shaped, sharp-pointed, often flexible, smooth, dark green, in clusters of two, evergreen. Cones 2-3 inches long, oval but much broader when opened, pale brown, growing in clusters at the tips of the branchlets, persisting; scales rounded, thickened, stiff, not armed with spines or prickles; seeds winged, smooth. Bark reddish brown, nearly smooth, becoming scaly. *Occurrence*: Widespread on both poor and rich soils in sandy areas. *Similar species*: Scrub pine (*P. banksiana*) and scotch pine (*P. sylvestris*) also bear needles in clusters of two, but those of the scrub pine are only 1½ inches long and those of the scotch pine are 2-3 inches long. *Comments*: Formerly known as *P. rubra*. Source of lumber. Although often called Norway pine, this is an American species.

PITCH PINE   PINE FAMILY
Pinus rigida   *Pinaceae*
                                                                   Plate 2, No. 2

Description: Tree 40-60 (sometimes 80 or more) feet tall, trunk straight or somewhat curved; branches irregular and spreading. Leaves 3-6 inches long, simple, needle-shaped, finely toothed, usually sharp-pointed, stiff, in groups of three, yellow-green, evergreen. Cones 2-3½ inches long, short and broad when open, pale brown, usually in clusters of 2-4 on the branchlets; scales thickened, usually with a stout, recurved prickle; seeds winged, smooth, blackish. Bark brownish gray, deeply furrowed into ridges or scales. *Occurrence*: Most commonly found on sandy soil or rocky slopes. *Similar species*: No other pine in the Adirondack area bears its needles in clusters of three. *Comments*: Also known as torch pine and candlewood pine. Excellent source of turpentine.

WHITE PINE   PINE FAMILY
Pinus strobus   *Pinaceae*
                                                                Plate 2, No. 3

Description: Tree 50-80 (occasionally 100 or more) feet tall, trunk straight, branches horizontal and whorled. Leaves 3-4 inches long, simple, needle-shaped, 3-sided, soft, clustered in groups of five, bluish green, partially coated with a whitish bloom, evergreen. Cones 4-6 inches long, cylindrical, slightly curved, dark brown when mature; scales blunt, thin, smooth; seeds winged, smooth. Bark pale greenish gray and smooth when young, becoming brown and somewhat roughened with age. *Occurrence*: Highly variable habitats, locally abundant. *Similar species*: No other pine in our area bears its needles in clusters of five. *Comments*: Largest northern conifer. Common source of lumber.

SCOTCH PINE   PINE FAMILY
Pinus sylvestris   *Pinaceae*
                                                                Plate 2, No. 4

Description: Tree 40-80 (sometimes 100 or more) feet tall, trunk straight; branches spreading. Leaves 1-3 inches long, simple, needle-shaped, stiff, twisted, in pairs, bluish green, smooth, evergreen. Cones 1-3 inches long, oval, yellowish brown to grayish brown, solitary or in pairs, hanging from the branchlets, tips pointing back towards main trunk, not persisting; scales with 4-sided recurving points, thickened at the tips, stiff, often with a hook-like extension; seeds winged, smooth. Bark on lower trunk grayish brown and scaly, upper trunk and large branches distinctly brownish orange. *Occurrence*: On rich moist soil, sandy habitats, and rocky slopes. *Similar species*: Scrub pine (*P. banksiana*) and red pine (*P. resinosa*) also bear their needles in clusters of two, but neither of these has the distinctly brownish orange bark of the scotch pine. *Comments*: Commonly cultivated as an ornamental. Also known as scots pine. Native to the Scottish highlands, escaped and established in some areas.

TAMARACK   PINE FAMILY
Larix laricina   *Pinaceae*
                                                     Plate 3, No. 1

Description: Tree 40-80 (occasionally up to 100) feet tall, trunk straight; branches spreading, foliage comparatively sparse. Leaves simple, growing in clusters of 8 or more, ½-1¼ inches long, needle-shaped, 3-sided, flexible, bluish green, becoming yellow-orange and falling in autumn. Cones about ½-¾ inch long, broadly oval, greenish when young, becoming purple-brown to brown in age, growing erect on the branches, persisting. Bark reddish brown, scaly. *Occurrence*: Widespread in swamps, bogs, and moist, rocky hillsides. *Similar species*: No other conifer bears its needles in such large clusters. *Comments*: Also known as American larch. Our only native conifer to completely shed its needles in the fall.

ARBOR VITAE   CEDAR FAMILY
Thuja occidentalis   *Cupressaceae*
                                                    Plate 3, No. 2

Description: Tree 20-65 (sometimes up to 80) feet tall, trunk swollen at the base, sometimes dividing into 2 or 3 parts; branches spreading. Leaves about ⅛ inch long, simple, opposite, scale-like, somewhat egg-shaped with a raised center, closely overlapping, aromatic when crushed, bright green overall, evergreen. Cones approximately ½ inch long, oval, woody, yellowish brown, usually erect, borne singly or in clusters along the branchlets, persisting through winter; scales 6-12, thin, oval; seeds about ⅛ inch long, oblong, winged. Bark grayish brown to reddish brown, fibrous, sometimes shredding. *Occurrence*: Common in low swampy areas, old pastures and mountain slopes. *Similar species*: Red cedar (*Juniperus virginiana*) also has scale-like, overlapping leaves, but they are only half the size of the above species. *Comments*: Also known as northern white cedar and swamp cedar. Used as a source of lumber for fence posts, shingles, and barrels. Frequently cultivated for hedges.

DWARF JUNIPER *Juniperus communis* var. *depressa*
CEDAR FAMILY
Cupressaceae
Plate 3, No. 3

Description: Shrub 1-3 feet tall growing in broad mats; branches radiating outward and upward. Leaves ⅓-½ inch long, needle-like, growing in whorls of three, spreading, sharp-pointed, dark green, evergreen. Cones ¼-⅜ inch in diameter, berry-like, nearly round, blue-gray, covered with a light colored bloom, resinous. Bark grayish brown. *Occurrence*: Widely distributed on poor rocky soil. *Similar species*: No other conifer bears needles in whorls of three. Both yew (*Taxus canadensis*) and hemlock (*Tsuga canadensis*) may have similar, shrubby outlines. *Comments*: Often found in rocky pastures. The berries of *J. communis* are used to flavor gin. Many species of wildlife feed on the cones.

EASTERN RED CEDAR *Juniperus virginiana*
CEDAR FAMILY
Cupressaceae
Plate 3, No. 4

Description: Tree 20-40 (sometimes 60 or more) feet tall, trunk straight; branches spreading. Leaves opposite in alternating pairs, growing in four rows, dark green, evergreen, of two kinds: (1) on young trees or new growth - needle-like, spreading from the branchlets, about ¼ inch long, stiff, sharp-pointed; (2) on older growth or mature trees - scale-like, overlapping, closely pressed to the branches, egg-shaped, about ¹⁄₁₆ inch long. Cones ¼-⅓ inch in diameter, berry-like, nearly round, fleshy, resinous, dark blue at maturity with a pale gray waxy bloom, containing 1-3 seeds. Bark reddish brown, fibrous, separating into long strands or just shredding. *Occurrence*: Found in sandy swamps, gravelly hillsides, and rocky slopes. *Similar species*: Arbor vitae (*Thuja occidentalis*) also has scale-like, overlapping leaves, but they are twice the size of those described above. *Comments*: Not of commercial significance because of limited quantity and slow growth rate.

RED SPRUCE   PINE FAMILY
Picea rubens   *Pinaceae*
Plate 4, No. 1

Description: Tree 60-80 (sometimes 100 or more) feet tall, trunk straight; branches spreading, with minutely hairy twigs (use hand lens). Leaves simple, densely covering all sides of the branchlets, approximately ½ inch long, needle-shaped, 4-sided, curved or straight, rigid, light green, evergreen. Cones 1-2 inches long, oval, woody, purplish brown to reddish brown, hanging from the branchlets, not persisting; scales rounded, thin, stiff, sometimes wavy, often 2-lobed; seeds winged, smooth, maturing in October. Bark reddish brown, scaly. *Occurrence*: Common in cool, moist habitats, widely distributed from low woodlands to the timberline of mountain slopes. *Similar species*: White spruce (*P. glauca* - was *P. canadensis*), is nearly identical to the red spruce, and occasionally occurs within the Adirondacks. It has slightly larger needles and cones, and smooth twigs. It is also known as cat spruce or skunk spruce because of the disagreeable odor of the needles when crushed. Norway spruce (*P. abies*), introduced from Europe, is easily identified by its oversized 4-7 inch cones. *Comments*: By far the commonest spruce of the Adirondacks. Frequently used as a Christmas tree.

BLACK SPRUCE   PINE FAMILY
Picea mariana   *Pinaceae*
Plate 4, No. 2

Description: Tree 20-50 (sometimes 60 or more) feet tall, trunk straight; branches numerous, irregular and rather short; with minutely hairy twigs. Leaves simple, densely covering all sides of the branchlets, ¼-½ inch long, needle-shaped, 4-sided, curved or straight, rigid, blue-green, evergreen. Cones ¾-1¼ inches long, broadly oval, woody, reddish brown, hanging from the branchlets, persistent; scales rounded or somewhat notched, thin, stiff; seeds winged, smooth. Bark grayish brown, scaly. *Occurrence*: Common in bogs and on mountain slopes. *Similar species*: No other spruce has such rounded cones or is typically found growing on bogs. *Comments*: Also known as bog spruce and swamp spruce. Important source of pulpwood. Twigs used to make spruce beer.

Section II

The Broad-Leaved Trees and Shrubs

Fire Cherry
Prunus penslyvanica, page 44

BALSAM POPLAR   WILLOW FAMILY
Populus balsamifera   *Salicaceae*
                                                       Plate 5, No. 1

Description: Tree 25-60 (sometimes 75) feet tall, trunk straight; with wide spreading branches. Leaves simple, alternate, 2½-5 inches long, oval with a tapering point, finely and roundly toothed, dark green on the upper surface, silvery white below, turning yellow in autumn; stalks about 1½ inches long, slender, slightly flattened. Flowers in May before the leaves unfold, in cylindrical catkins 3-5 inches long. Fruit many small oval, 2-valved capsules, borne along drooping catkins 4-6 inches long; seeds light brown, hairy, ripening in late spring. Bark smooth and brownish when young, becoming gray, rough. *Occurrence*: Found on river banks and in wet areas. *Similar species*: The bark might be mistaken for that of the aspens, but none of these has leaves with long, tapering tips. *Comments*: The buds have a pleasant, spicy fragrance.

COTTONWOOD   WILLOW FAMILY
Populus deltoides   *Salicaceae*
                                                       Plate 5, No. 2

Description: Tree 50-80 (sometimes 90 or more) feet tall, trunk straight; lower branches level, upper branches ascending. Leaves simple, alternate, 3-6 inches long, almost as wide, triangular with a tapering point, edged with small curved, wave-like teeth, shiny green above, pale green below, turning yellow in autumn; stalks long, slender, flattened. Flowers in May before the leaves unfold, in drooping catkins 2½-7 inches long. Fruit many 2-4 valved capsules, bead-like, almost ½ inch long, borne along drooping catkins 5-10 inches long; seeds light brown, cottony, ripening in late June. Bark gray, becoming rough and darkening with age. *Occurrence*: Prefers rich, moist soils from stream borders to swamp edges. *Similar species*: The black or lombardy poplar (*P. nigra*), planted as an ornamental, has similar but less distinctly toothed leaves. This Eurasian import never produces female flowers or fruit. *Comments*: Previously known as *P. monilifera*. Locally known as the necklace poplar, named for the visual similarity of the unripe fruiting catkins to a large beaded necklace.

LARGE-TOOTHED ASPEN WILLOW FAMILY
Populus grandidentata Salicaceae
Plate 5, No. 3

Description: Tree 30-50 (sometimes 80) feet tall, trunk straight; branches gently ascending. Leaves simple, alternate, 3-5 inches long, broadly egg-shaped, tip pointed, edged with large, irregular, dull pointed teeth, dark green above, pale green below, turning yellow in autumn; leafstalks long, slender, flattened. Flowers in April, in drooping catkins 1½-4 inches long. Fruit many small 2-valved capsules, borne along drooping catkins 3-4 inches long; seeds tiny, dark brown, cottony, ripening in late May. Bark greenish gray, becoming brown and roughening. *Occurrence*: Variable, ranging from the borders of wet areas to dry hillsides. *Similar species*: The trunk of the trembling aspen (*P. tremuloides*) is very similar, especially when viewed in winter, but this species has nearly round leaves with tiny teeth. *Comments*: The last of our poplars to set leaves. When first appearing the leaves are distinctly silvery, providing a pleasing contrast to its greener surroundings.

TREMBLING ASPEN WILLOW FAMILY
Populus tremuloides Salicaceae
Plate 5, No. 4

Description: Tree 20-40 (occasionally 50 or more) feet tall, trunk straight; branches ascending. Leaves simple, alternate, 1½-2½ inches long, nearly round with a sharp point, margin finely toothed, dark green on the upper surface, dull and pale green below, turning bright yellow in autumn; stalks long, flattened, slender. Flowers in April, in drooping catkins 1½-3 inches long. Fruit many small 2-valved capsules, each about ¼ inch long, borne along drooping catkins about 4 inches long; seeds pale brown, cottony, ripening in May. Bark greenish gray with dark patches forming beneath the limbs, darkening with age. *Occurrence*: Widespread on most soils except swampy habitats. *Similar species*: The trunk and bark of the large-toothed aspen (*P. grandidentata*) are very similar, but this species has egg-shaped leaves with very large teeth. *Comments*: The most widespread hardwood in North America. Also known as the American aspen and quaking aspen.

THE TREE-SIZED WILLOWS*

BLACK WILLOW   WILLOW FAMILY
Salix nigra   *Salicaceae*
Plate 6, Nos. 3 & 4

Description: Tree 25-40 (occasionally 50 or more) feet tall, often with multiple trunks which are short, stout, usually crooked, frequently inclined; branches ascending and spreading. Leaves simple, alternate, 1½-5 (usually 2-3) inches long, thinly lance-shaped with a rounded base, tips long-pointed, margin finely toothed, bright green and shiny above, paler beneath; stipules prominent on new growth. Flowers occur in catkins 1-3 inches long, and are the last of our native willows to bloom. Fruit many small, reddish brown capsules arranged along a common stalk, catkin-like, ripe in the late spring. Bark blackish brown, deeply grooved, rough. *Occurrence*: Moist or wet habitats, stream banks, lakeshores. *Similar species*: The crack willow (*S. fragilis*), introduced from Europe, has similar leaves with the differences of a tapering base, coarser teeth and small stipules. The common name refers to a characteristic brittleness of the twigs. The white willow (*S. alba*) is another tree-sized introduction from Europe. The common name refers to the pale appearance of the tree, caused by a dense coat of silvery white hairs covering both sides of the leaves. This species is most easily located in the spring, when its bright yellow branch tips are most evident. *Comments*: Also known as swamp willow. The largest of our native willows.

---

*The willows form a large and complex group. Similarity of species and frequent hybridization make a complete workup on this genus beyond the scope of this book. Those willows listed here include our commonest and most distinctive species, but many additional species also inhabit the Adirondacks. The distinction between tree-sized and shrub-sized willows employed here is an artificial classification adopted purely for the sake of convenience.

THE SHRUB-SIZED WILLOWS

PUSSY WILLOW
Salix discolor

WILLOW FAMILY
Salicaceae
Plate 6, No. 1

Description: Usually a shrub or occasionally a small tree, 5-15 (sometimes 25) feet tall, trunk short and bearing stout ascending branches. Leaves simple, alternate, 3-5 inches long, broadly lance-shaped with a tapering base, tips pointed, margins irregularly toothed, green and smooth on the upper surface, silvery white below. Flowers appear in spring before the leaves unfold, in furry, cylindrical catkins about 1-2 inches long. Fruit many small, pale brown, long-beaked capsules arranged along a common stalk, ripe in late spring. Bark greenish brown. *Occurrence*: Wet habitats, such as streambanks, swamps, drainage ditches and lakeshores. *Similar species*: The shining willow (*S. lucida*) has smooth twigs and leaves with rounded bases, extended tips, and is smooth on both surfaces. It often forms thickets along waterways. The heart-leaved willow (*S. cordata*) also forms thickets in similar situations. Its twigs are covered with a pale gray downiness. The leaves are broader, short-pointed and sometimes heart-shaped at the base. The leaves of the goat willow (*S. caprea*) are egg-shaped, have a pale gray hairiness beneath, and minute teeth near the tip. This species was introduced from Europe. The bearberry willow (*S. uva-ursi*) is our shortest willow. It is found only at high altitudes and in Alpine regions. Its leaves are only ½-¾ inch long, and dark green. *Comments*: Freshly emerging flowers covered with silky hairs are commonly picked for flower arrangements.

BITTERNUT HICKORY
Carya cordiformis

WALNUT FAMILY
Juglandaceae

Description: Tree 50-75 (sometimes 80) feet tall, trunk straight, long, stout; branches ascending and spreading; twigs ending in bright yellow, slightly flattened buds. Leaves pinnate-compound, alternate, 6-10 inches long, 5-11 (usually 9) leaflets, lower leaflets smaller, leaflets broadly to thinly lance-shaped, tips pointed, margin saw-toothed, bright green on the upper surface, paler beneath, turning yellow in autumn. Flowers bloom in May, in triple-clustered catkins 3-4 inches long. Fruit ¾-1¼ inches long, oval, maturing in September; husk green with yellowish glandular dots on the surface, splitting into 4 wings; nut nearly round, buff colored, sharp-pointed, thin-shelled; kernel reddish brown, bitter. Bark pale gray to grayish brown, roughened. *Occurrence*: Stream banks, fields, and wooded slopes. *Similar species*: Easily differentiated from all other hickories by the bright yellow buds on the twig tips. *Comments*: The kernels are too bitter to be eaten. Bitternuts found in the Adirondacks have a thicker husk than those gathered in other parts of its range.

PIGNUT HICKORY
Carya glabra

WALNUT FAMILY
Juglandaceae
Plate 7, No. 2

Description: Tree 50-60 (sometimes 80 or more) feet tall, trunk slender, slightly tapering; branches ascending and spreading. Leaves pinnate-compound, alternate, 8-12 inches long, 5-7 leaflets, the lower leaflets distinctly smaller and lance-shaped, tips pointed, margins finely saw-toothed and hairless, yellow-green above, paler beneath, turning yellow in autumn. Flowers bloom in May, in triple-clustered catkins 3-4 inches long. Fruit 1-1½ inches long, oval, maturing in September; husk greenish brown, splitting halfway into 4 sections when mature; nut about 1 inch long, oval, flattened, sharp-pointed, pale brown, covered with a hard shell; kernel sweet when young, becoming bitter, difficult to extract. Bark dark gray, roughened by shallow grooves and ridges. *Occurrence*: Dry ridges and slopes, also in swampy habitats. *Similar species*: Shagbark hickory (*C. ovata*) has similar leaves which may be differentiated by their minutely hairy margins.

SHAGBARK HICKORY
Carya ovata

WALNUT FAMILY
Juglandaceae
Plate 7, No. 1

Description: Tree 50-70 (sometimes 80 or more) feet tall, trunk straight, slender; branches stout and spreading. Leaves pinnate-compound, alternate, 8-14 inches long, usually 5 leaflets, upper leaflets very broad, tips pointed, margins finely toothed and minutely hairy, dark green on the upper surface, pale green beneath, turning yellow in autumn. Flowers bloom in May in drooping catkins 4-5 inches long. Fruit 1-2 inches long, globular, ripening in September and October; husk about ½ inch thick, dark brown, separating into 4 wings at maturity; nut globular, pointed, slightly flattened, buff white, thin-shelled; kernel large, sweet, edible. Bark pale gray and smooth on young trunks, becoming dark brown-gray and remarkably shaggy on older specimens. *Occurrence*: Wooded hillsides. *Similar species*: Pignut hickory (*C. glabra*) has similar leaves which may be differentiated by the lack of minute hairs on their margins. *Comments*: Formerly known as *Hicoria ovata*. Frequently found growing with white oak.

BUTTERNUT
Juglans cinerea

WALNUT FAMILY
Juglandaceae
Plate 7, No. 3

Description: Tree 40-60 (sometimes 80 or more) feet tall, trunk short, straight, dividing; branches horizontal, ascending. Leaves pinnate-compound, alternate, 15-30 inches long; leaflets 9-17 (commonly 11), toothed, yellow-green, somewhat downy beneath, turning yellow in autumn; stalks hairy, sticky. Flowers bloom in May, in drooping catkins 3-5 inches long. Fruit 1½-3 inches long, cylindrical, in clusters of 3-5, ripening in September; husk yellow-brown when mature, hairy, sticky, staining, not splitting into sections; nut cylindrical, pointed, deeply furrowed, thick-shelled; kernel large, oily, edible. Bark pale gray, furrowed. *Occurrence*: Prefers low rich woods and hillsides. *Similar species*: The black walnut, (*J. nigra*) has very dark, nearly black bark, a round husk, and more and smaller leaflets. Our survey found native black walnut growing near, but not in, the Adirondack Park. *Comments*: Also known as white walnut and oilnut. The name butternut refers to the extremely oily kernel.

SPECKLED ALDER BIRCH FAMILY
Alnus rugosa *Betulaceae*
Plate 8, No. 1

Description: Shrub or small tree 8-15 (sometimes 20) feet tall. Leaves 3-4 inches long, simple, alternate, broadly oval and sometimes slightly asymmetrical, sharply and irregularly double toothed, tips pointed, dull green above, often downy beneath. Flowers bloom late April or May before the leaves unfold, in drooping catkins 2-3 inches long. Fruit a cone, ½-¾ inch long, oval, woody, dark colored, persisting; seeds round, winged, maturing in autumn. Bark gray, speckled with tiny white spots which give this alder its name. *Occurrence*: Found in wet soils along swamps and streams. *Similar species*: The European black alder (*A. glutinosa*) is much larger, growing to heights of 50-70 feet. It has escaped cultivation and is establishing itself. The leaves resemble those of the speckled alder, except that the tips are either blunt or notched inward. The mountain alder (*A. crispa*) is a shrub alder growing only at much higher elevations. *Comments*: Was *A. incana*.

YELLOW BIRCH BIRCH FAMILY
Betula alleghaniensis *Betulaceae*
Plate 8, No. 4

Description: Tree 50-70 (occasionally 80 or more) feet tall, trunk short, often dividing near the base; branches ascending, with drooping tips. Leaves 3-5 inches long, simple, alternate (often alternate in pairs), egg-shaped with a slight point, margin coarsely double-toothed, dull dark green on the upper surface, yellow-green below, turning yellow in autumn. Flowers in late May, male flowers in drooping catkins 3-4 inches long, female flowers in upright catkins about 1 inch high. Fruit erect, cone-like, 1-1½ inches tall, egg-shaped; made up of hairy 3-lobed scales enclosing small 2-winged nutlets. Bark lustrous, yellowish brown, peeling horizontally. *Occurrence*: Common on moist soil along stream banks, swamps and slopes. *Similar species*: Black birch (*B. lenta*) has similar leaves, shiny dark reddish brown bark that does not peel off, and hairless scales on the fruit. *Comments*: Formerly known as *B. lutea*. Freshly broken twigs of both the yellow and the black birch have an odor of wintergreen, giving rise to the shared common name of "sweet birch."

PAPER BIRCH
Betula papyrifera

BIRCH FAMILY
Betulaceae
Plate 8, No. 3

Description: Tree 40-70 feet tall, trunk often angled away from the hillside, lower branches horizontal, upper branches ascending. Leaves 2-4 inches long, simple, alternate, oval to egg-shaped (heart-shaped at higher altitudes), long-pointed, coarsely toothed, dark green above, light green below, turning yellow in autumn. Flowers in spring before the leaves unfold, in drooping catkins 1½-3½ inches long. Fruit drooping, cone-like, 1½-2 inches long; made up of smooth 3-lobed scales with hairy margins, enclosing small double winged nutlets, maturing in autumn. Bark on trunk and large limbs creamy white, smooth, separating into horizontal strips; new growth glossy reddish black. *Occurrence*: Hillsides and often in previously burned areas. *Similar species*: The gray birch (*B. populifolia*) also has light colored bark, but it has triangular leaves and non-peeling bark. The ornamental white birch (*B. pendula*) is a European import with more triangular leaves that has not escaped into the wild. *Comments*: Also known as the white birch. Previously known as *B. alba* var. *papyrifera*. Once used to make canoes because of the waterproof nature of the bark. Removal of the bark kills the tree.

GRAY BIRCH
Betula populifolia

BIRCH FAMILY
Betulaceae

Description: Tree 15-30 (occasionally 45) feet tall, branches spreading, often growing in groups. Leaves 2-3 inches long, simple, alternate (often alternate in pairs), triangular, long-pointed, sharply toothed along an uneven margin, dark glossy green above, paler beneath, turning yellow in autumn. Flowers in spring before the leaves unfold, in drooping catkins ¼-4 inches long. Fruit drooping, cone-like, ¾-1 inch long; made up of hairy 3-lobed scales enclosing small, double-winged nutlets. Bark grayish white, smooth, marked by triangular dark patches beneath the branches, not peeling. *Occurrence*: Variable, found on poor soils, rocky slopes, swampy depressions, and wooded hill-sides. *Similar species*: Paper birch (*B. papyrifera*) has white peeling bark and oval to heart-shaped leaves.

BEAKED HAZELNUT
Corylus cornuta

BIRCH FAMILY
Betulaceae
Plate 9, No. 4

Description: Shrub 4-8 feet tall, trunk straight, dividing; branches ascending, spreading, forming small thickets. Leaves 2-6 inches long, simple, alternate, broadly oval, abruptly pointed, very irregularly double-toothed, bright green on the upper surface, paler below. Flowers of two kinds, male in drooping catkins, female scarlet, very small, blooming in early May. Fruit completely surrounded by tubular, leaf-like bracts covered with irritating, bristly hairs, often occurring in pairs; nut oval, brown, smooth, moderately thin-shelled, with a large, sweet, edible kernel; ripening from late August to early September. Bark yellow-brown, smooth. *Occurrence*: The edges of woodlands, wooded streams, and on hillsides. *Similar species*: American hazelnut (*C. americana*) is far less common, and the bracts of its fruit do not become long and tubular. *Comments*: Formerly known as *C. rostrata*.

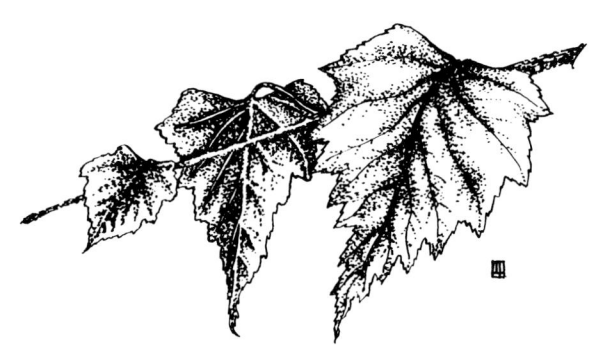

Gray Birch
Betula populifolia, page 31

AMERICAN HORNBEAM BIRCH FAMILY
Carpinus caroliniana *Betulaceae*
Plate 9, No. 2

Description: Small tree 10-20 (sometimes 30 or more) feet tall, trunk straight or curved, dividing; branches long, slender, ascending and drooping at the tips. Leaves 2-4 inches long, simple, alternate, oblong with a pointed tip, often asymmetrical, sharply double-toothed, dull green on the upper surface, paler below, turning brilliant orange to scarlet in autumn. Flowers bloom in May, in drooping catkins about 1½ inches long. Fruit a drooping cluster about 3 inches long, made up of 3-lobed, leaf-like bracts, each enclosing a single small corrugated nut, ripening in September. Bark bluish gray tinged with brown, vertically ridged. *Occurrence*: Swamps, the banks of streams, and on moist slopes. *Similar species*: Young beech (*Fagus grandifolia*) has similar bark but leaves with larger, more evenly spaced teeth. *Comments*: Also known as blue beech, musclewood, or water beech. The texture of the trunk resembles hard, highly developed muscles.

EASTERN HOPHORNBEAM BIRCH FAMILY
Ostraya virginiana *Betulaceae*
Plate 9, No. 1

Description: Tree 20-30 (sometimes 50) feet tall, trunk straight or curved, dividing; branches ascending and spreading. Leaves 3-5 inches long, simple, alternate, oblong, tapering to a point, often asymmetrical, sharply double-toothed, dull green on the upper surface, paler below, turning yellow in autumn. Flowers blooming in April or May, in drooping catkins about 2 inches long, usually in groups of 3. Fruit a cone-like drooping cluster, 2-3 inches long, resembling those of the hop vine, made up of inflated, overlapping papery scales which are protected by irritating, cactus-like spines; each scale contains a single, hard, flattened nutlet which ripens from late August through September. Bark grayish brown, scaly. *Occurrence*: Dry gravelly slopes. *Similar species*: The American hornbeam (*Carpinus caroliniana*) has much smoother bark, and fruit which has flat, not inflated, scales. *Comments*: Also known as ironwood because of its hardness and strength.

AMERICAN CHESTNUT   BEECH FAMILY
Castanea dentata   *Fagaceae*
Plate 10, No. 1

Description: Formerly a tree 50-100 feet tall with a massive trunk and heavy ascending branches, now reduced by blight to short-lived and slender specimens rarely reaching 15 feet tall. Leaves simple, alternate, 6-9 inches long, narrowly oval, tips pointed, large and evenly spaced teeth along the margin, dark shiny green above, paler green beneath, becoming bronze yellow in autumn. Flowers bloom in July, many in thin, downy, and often erect catkins 6-8 inches long; individual flowers creamy white, without petals, about ¼ inch in diameter. Fruit a sharply spined burr, 2-3 inches in diameter, splitting into 4 sections when ripe, enclosing 2-3 nuts; individual nuts roundly wedge-shaped, slightly flattened, almost 1 inch in diameter, tips pointed and downy white; shell ruddy brown; kernel large, easily extracted, sweet, edible, maturing in September and October. (This describes a healthy nut. Most specimens at this time are producing hollow, sterile nuts.) Bark grayish brown, roughened. *Occurrence*: In rich soils along farmlands and in woods. *Similar species*: The leaves appear very similar to those of the American beech (*Fagus grandifolia*), but these are much smaller leaves growing on a much larger tree. *Comments*: Never common throughout the park, the chestnut did occur in numbers along the eastern borders until descimated by the European chestnut blight. Survivors are seen only as saplings springing up from the old roots. These live about 10 years, then die back to ground level and the cycle repeats. These specimens do flower and fruit, but it is only in the final year before they die back that they are likely to produce healthy nuts.

AMERICAN BEECH BEECH FAMILY
Fagus grandifolia *Fagaceae*
Plate 10, No. 2

Description: Tree 45-60 (occasionally 80 or more) feet tall, trunk straight; branches stout, horizontal or ascending. Leaves 3-5 inches long, simple, alternate, oval, stiff, sharply pointed, distinctly and evenly toothed, light green above, paler below, turning golden yellow in autumn, becoming coppery and often persisting through winter. Flowers bloom in May, inconspicuous, often unobservable due to the height of mature trees. Fruit a prickled burr, about ¾ inch long, opening in 4 sections, usually containing 2 nuts; nuts ½-¾ inch long, 3-sided, shell brown, smooth, shining; kernel large, easily extracted, sweet, edible, maturing in early September. Bark light gray, smooth, unbroken. *Occurrence*: Moist bottom lands, rich uplands, and gravelly slopes. *Similar species*: American hornbeam (*Carpinus caroliniana*) has smooth gray bark, but is much shorter. *Comments*: Excellent source of hardwood lumber. Also known as white beech. The edible fruit is commonly called a beechnut. Most authorities advise roasting the nuts before eating. The widespread practice of carving names and dates on the bark can kill these noble trees.

THE WHITE OAKS

WHITE OAK **BEECH FAMILY**
Quercus alba *Fagaceae*
Plate 11, No. 1

Description: Tree 60-80 (sometimes 100 or more) feet tall, trunk stout, straight, dividing; branches large, spreading. Leaves simple, alternate, 5-9 inches long, reverse egg-shaped with usually 5-9 broad, deeply cut, rounded lobes, bright green above, paler beneath, turning reddish bronze in fall, often persisting into winter. Flowers bloom in May, in drooping catkins 2-3 inches long. Fruit short-stalked acorns, usually occurring in pairs; the cup shallow, rough; the nut ¾-1 inch long, oval to egg-shaped, pale brown; the kernel large, sweet, edible, maturing in September. Bark light gray, with shallow fissures. *Occurrence*: Grows in a wide variety of soils, including rich uplands, moist bottom lands, sandy plains and gravelly slopes. *Similar species*: Other white oaks (oaks with rounded lobes on their leaves) are the swamp white oak and the chestnut oak. The swamp white oak (*Q. bicolor*) has leaves broadest above the middle, with 5-6 shallow and usually uneven lobes along each side. The acorns, often in pairs, have stems 1¼-3 inches long. The chestnut oak (*Q. prinus*) has leaves with about 10 shallow, rounded teeth along each side, looking very much like a dull-toothed chestnut leaf. The acorns are borne on short stems under ½ inch long. Both of these oaks are found mainly along eastern waterways in the park, the white oak has a wider distribution. The burr oak (*Q. macrocarpa*) has been reported in literature from the northwest corner of the Adirondack Park. *Comments*: The white oak is often found growing in association with shagbark hickory.

THE RED OAKS

NORTHERN RED OAK   BEECH FAMILY
Quercus rubra   *Fagaceae*
Plate 10, No. 3

Description: Tree 50-80 (occasionally 100 or more) feet tall, trunk stout, straight; branches ascending and spreading. Leaves simple, alternate, 5-9 inches long, oval in outline, usually with 7-11 shallow lobes, each lobe with 1-3 bristle-tipped teeth, dull dark green above, paler beneath, turning dark red in fall. Flowers bloom in May, in drooping catkins 4-5 inches long. Fruit very short-stalked acorns; cup usually shallow, finely scaled; nut oblong to egg-shaped, about 1 inch long, reddish brown; kernel large, white, very bitter, maturing in September. Bark dark brown, roughened by fissures and wide ridges. *Occurrence*: Found in a variety of habitats, including rich woods, and sandy or gravelly soils. *Similar species*: Another red oak (oaks with sharply pointed lobes on their leaves) is the black oak (*Q. velutina*), found along the southwest edge of the Adirondack Park. It has variable leaves, often similar to those of the northern red oak, with the difference that they are glossy on the upper surface. The acorn is often enclosed for half its length in a deep cup. *Comments*: Excellent source of hardwood lumber. The tallest and most rapid growing of all oak species. This is the most widespread oak within the park, and the only one whose range extends up into the High Peaks.

HACKBERRY
Celtis occidentalis

ELM FAMILY
Ulmaceae
Plate 12, No. 2

Description: Tree 25-60 (sometimes 80 or more) feet tall, trunk short, straight, dividing; branches spreading. Leaves 2-4 inches long, simple, alternate, triangular with distinctly uneven sides, tip long and tapering, coarsely toothed except near the base, light green and rough on the upper surface, paler and usually smooth below. Flowers pale green, inconspicuous, appearing with the first leaves. Fruit ¼-½ inch in diameter, solitary, drooping on long stalks from base of leaf stems, purple-brown, 1-seeded; flesh thin, orange, sweet, edible, ripening in September, sometimes persisting through fall. Bark grayish brown, with corky warts. *Occurrence*: Rich moist soil, also in gravelly uplands. *Similar species*: Sometimes mistaken for an elm (*Ulmus americana*) but differentiated by its fruit, which is a flat, winged key. *Comments*: Also known as nettle-tree, false elm and sugar-berry.

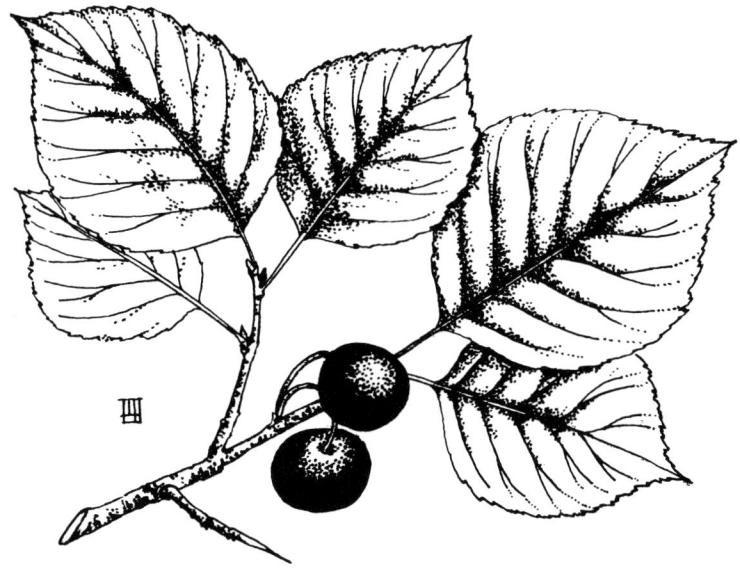

Canada Plum
Prunus nigra, page 43

AMERICAN ELM
Ulmus americana

ELM FAMILY
Ulmaceae
Plate 11, No. 4

Description: Tree 75-100 (occasionally 120) feet tall, trunk stout, straight, dividing into several secondary trunks; branches large, ascending. Leaves 4-6 inches long, simple, alternate, oval with distinctly uneven sides, tapering to a sharp point, coarsely double-toothed, dark green and usually rough on the upper surface, paler and usually smooth below, turning bright yellow in autumn; stalks short, smooth. Flowers in clusters, green, inconspicuous, blooming in spring before the leaves appear. Fruit in long-stemmed clusters; individual keys ½ inch long, flat, oval with a distinctly notched tip, winged, smooth on both sides, hairy on the margin, 1-seeded, ripening in June. Bark gray, rough. *Occurrence*: Bottomlands, along streams, and bordering lakes and ponds. *Similar species*: Most large American elms have now died from Dutch elm disease, making any healthy sighting most likely the slippery elm (*U. rubra*) or rarely the cork elm (*U. thomasii*). *Comments*: Also known as white elm and water elm. Usually found as a large standing skeleton.

SLIPPERY ELM
Ulmus rubra

ELM FAMILY
Ulmaceae
Plate 12, No. 1

Description: Tree 30-50 (occasionally 70 or more) feet tall, trunk short, stout, dividing; branches thick, ascending and spreading. Leaves 5-7 inches long, simple, alternate, broadly oval with distinctly uneven sides, tapering to a sharp point, coarsely double-toothed, dark green above, paler beneath, rough on both surfaces, turning bright yellow in autumn; stalks short, rough. Flowers in clusters, green, inconspicuous, blooming in spring before the leaves appear. Fruit in short-stalked clusters; individual keys ½-¾ inch long, flat, nearly round, winged, smooth on both sides, margin hairless, 1-seeded, ripening in June. Bark dark brown, rough. *Occurrence*: Along streams and on hillsides. *Similar species*: Although rare in the north, you may encounter the cork elm (*U. thomasii*, originally *U. racemosa*) which differs by having hairy fruit and twigs which sport thick, corky wings. *Comments*: Formerly known as *U. fulva*.

GOOSEBERRIES AND CURRANTS
Ribes sp.

GOOSEBERRY FAMILY
Grossulariaceae
Plate 12, Nos. 3 & 4

Nine species of currants and gooseberries live within the Adirondack Park. Despite their similarities, with a little practice it becomes easy to differentiate species. The following general description and specific key will assist you in this task.

Description: Shrub 1-5 feet tall, with numerous stems and branches. Leaves simple, alternate, 1-3 inches long, maple-like with 3-5 lobes, lobe tips pointed, margin irregularly toothed, dark green. Flowers bloom in May and June, usually in drooping clusters along a central stalk. Fruit red, reddish purple or black, round, ¼-½ inch in diameter, surface smooth or armed with hair-like prickles, pleasant tasting in most species, maturing in late summer. Bark gray to brown, smooth or spined, sometimes shredding. *Occurrence*: Rich woodlands, especially hardwoods, also open rocky fields; found at all elevations.

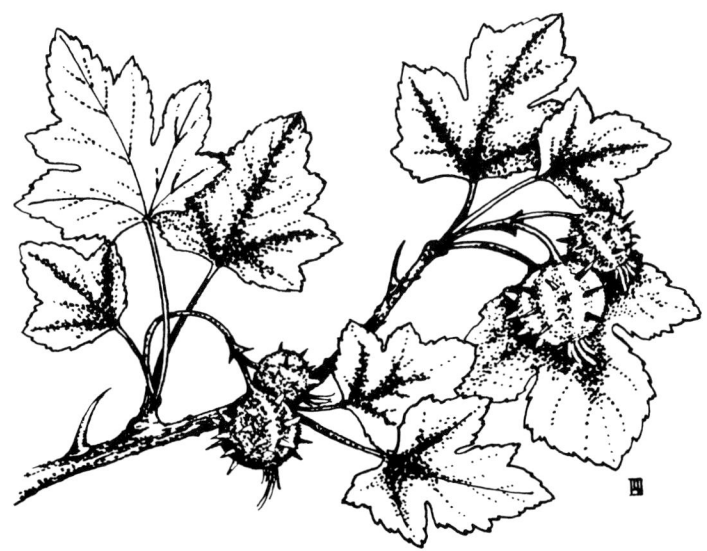

Common Gooseberry
Ribes cynosbati

Key to the Currants and Gooseberries

I. The Currants: Stems lacking spines or prickles (except *R. lacustre*). Usually flowers and fruits in clusters of 4 to 8 or more.
   A. Mature fruit black.
        1. Fruit surface smooth. Bruised twigs without an unpleasant odor. *R. americanum*.
        2. Fruit surface smooth. Bruised twigs with an offensive odor. *R. nigrum* (introduced from Europe).
        3. Fruit surface armed with hairlike prickles. *R. lacustre* (The only true currant to have stems armed with spines.)
   B. Mature fruit red.
        1. Fruit surface smooth. Leaf margins minutely hairy (use hand lens). *R. triste*.
        2. Fruit surface smooth. Leaf margins not minutely hairy. *R. sativum* (introduced from Europe).
        3. Fruit surface armed with prickles. *R. glandulosum*.

II. The Gooseberries: Stems armed with spines or prickles. Usually flowers and fruits either singly or in groups of 2 to 3.
   A. Mature fruit reddish purple.
        1. Fruit surface armed with prickles. *R. cynosbati*.
   B. Mature fruit blue-black to black.
        1. Fruit surface smooth. Leaves 1½-2½ inches long, sharply toothed. *R. hirtellum*.
        2. Fruit surface smooth. Leaves under 1 inch long, with few rounded teeth. *R. odoratum* (Introduced from western U.S.). Unique among *Ribes* by having tubular yellow flowers with a very spicy fragrance.

COMMON JUNEBERRY ROSE FAMILY
Amelanchier laevis *Rosaceae*
Plate 13, Nos. 1 & 2

Description: Shrub or small tree 15-25 feet tall, with a single trunk and ascending branches. Leaves simple, alternate, 1-2½ inches long, oval, margin evenly and finely toothed, tips pointed, dark green above, paler beneath, turning yellow in autumn. Flowers bloom in May, in open clusters; individual flowers white, with 5 elongated petals about ¾ inch long and ¼ inch wide. Fruit looks like a large blueberry, ½-¾ inch long, purple, long-stemmed, several in an open cluster; flesh juicy, edible, with several seeds, maturing in July and August. Bark gray, smooth. *Occurrence*: Roadsides and young woods. *Similar species*: Several other species of juneberries inhabit the Adirondacks. Most are very similar, and making positive identification can be very difficult. Among the most common of the other species are the following: downy juneberry (*A. arborea*) occurs as a clustered shrub or small tree. The fruit is dry and lacks flavor. Found in open woodlots and along streams. Bartram's juneberry (*A. bartramiana*) is a shrub 2-8 feet tall. It differs from other juneberries by having flowers and fruit occurring either solitary or in very small clusters. It is found along bogs and in acid soils. The round-leaved juneberry (*A. sanguinea*) is a straggling shrub 3-8 feet tall. Despite the common name, the leaves are only broadly oval. The fruit is among the best of any juneberry in flavor. It is found along lakeshores and in rocky or sandy soils. Its Latin name refers to the red color of the young twigs. *Comments*: Also known as serviceberries or shadberries. The latter name refers to the coincidence that in some areas of the country the flowering season matches the shad's spawning runs. Despite the common name of juneberry, within the park the fruit does not ripen until July.

THE HAWTHORNS
Crataegus sp.

ROSE FAMILY
Rosaceae
Plate 15, No. 1

Crataegus is a large genus comprising a great number of very similar species. It takes an experienced specialist to differentiate among the species, and there is little agreement among the experts as to just how many species comprise this genus. The hawthorns are well represented throughout most of the Adirondack Park, and may be identified by the following general description.

Description: Shrub or small tree 15-25 (sometimes 30 or more) feet tall, with irregular, spreading branches and many sharp thorns 1-3 inches long. Leaves simple, alternate, 1½-3 inches long, broad, usually with several shallow lobes, very coarsely and irregularly toothed, tips pointed, dark green above, paler beneath, turning yellow to red in autumn. Flowers bloom in May, in attractive spherical clusters; individual flowers white, ¾-1 inch wide, with five round petals, ill-scented. Fruit usually red, sometimes orange-red, nearly spherical, apple-like, ¼-¾ inch long; flesh dry and mealy, edible, enclosing 1-5 (usually 5) seeds, maturing in September. Bark brown to gray, scaly. *Occurrence*: Open to lightly wooded hillsides. *Similar species*: None. *Comments*: Also called "Thorns."

CANADA PLUM
Prunus nigra

ROSE FAMILY
Rosaceae

Description: Shrub or small tree 6-12 (sometimes 25) feet tall, with irregularly angled branches, armed with thorn-like twigs about 1 inch long. Leaves simple, alternate, broadly oval, short-tapered at tip, margin doubly and roundly toothed, olive green above, paler beneath, with 2 dark red glands near the base of the blade. Flowers bloom in May, before the leaves unfold, in umbrella-shaped clusters; individual flowers about 1 inch broad, with 5 rounded petals, petals white, often pink tinged at base. Fruit oval to nearly round, about 1 inch in diameter, dull red, thick-skinned; flesh juicy, edible, sour (taste greatly improved when early frost occurs), enclosing a single, oval, flattened seed, maturing in late summer. Bark brownish gray. *Occurrence*: In thickets, along stream and river banks. *Similar species*: The wild plum (*P. americana*) has sharply toothed leaves and orangish red fruit.

FIRE CHERRY ROSE FAMILY
Prunus penslyvanica *Rosaceae*
Description: Small tree 15-20 (occasionally 30 or more) feet tall, trunk straight, thin, with ascending and spreading branches. Leaves 3-5 inches long, simple, alternate, thinly lance-shaped, finely toothed, bright green and shiny on the upper surface, paler below; stalks short. Flowers ½ inch in diameter, with 5 rounded white petals, borne in long-stalked clusters of 4-5, blooming in May and June. Fruit round, ¼ inch in diameter, bright red, flesh sour, enclosing a single oblong stone, borne in clusters like the flowers; ripening in July and August. Bark reddish brown, nearly smooth, peeling off in papery strips. *Occurrence*: Rocky soils, burned areas and hillsides. *Similar species*: The Eurasian mazzard cherry (*P. avium*) also bears flowers and fruit in clusters but has a thick irregular trunk, broader leaves, and much larger fruit. This introduced species can be found on long abandoned farms and hedgerows within the Adirondacks. *Comments*: Also known as pin cherry. Although small, the pitted fruit is edible and superior in quality to the choke cherry.

SAND CHERRY ROSE FAMILY
Prunus pumila *Rosaceae*
Description: Shrub 1-5 feet tall, with stems often prostrate and spreading in form. Leaves simple, alternate, 1½-2½ inches long, paddle or bluntly lance-shaped, margin toothed along upper portion, olive green above, paler beneath, turning red in autumn. Flowers bloom in May or June with the first leaves, in few flowered clusters; individual flowers ¼ - ⅜ inch wide, with 5 white, rounded petals. Fruit borne in small hanging clusters; individual fruit almost round, about ½ inch long, reddish black; flesh thin, edible but usually very sour, enclosing a single, large, oval seed, maturing in late summer. Bark brown-gray, rough; newer growth shining and reddish. *Occurrence*: In sandy or rocky soils, especially shores and moist areas. *Similar species*: No other member of this family grows from often prostrate stems. *Comments*: A small and often overlooked species.

RUM CHERRY ROSE FAMILY
Prunus serotina *Rosaceae*
Plate 14, No. 4

Description: Tree 25-60 (sometimes 90 or more) feet tall, trunk stout, dividing to form several spreading branches. Leaves 2-5 inches long, simple, alternate, lance-shaped, finely toothed, dark green and shiny on the upper surface, paler below, short-stalked. Flowers about ¼ inch in diameter, white, with 5 rounded petals, borne in clusters 3-4 inches long, blooming in early June. Fruit purplish black, round, ½ inch in diameter, borne in drooping clusters; each containing a single round seed; ripening late August through September with a few persisting well into October. Bark reddish brown becoming brownish black and roughened with age. *Occurrence*: Rich soils, especially on slopes. *Similar species*: Choke cherry (*P. virginiana*) is smaller, often only a bush, and has red, astringent fruit and broader leaves. *Comments*: Pitted fruit edible and historically used to flavor rum. Favorite food of black bears and many bird species.

CHOKE CHERRY ROSE FAMILY
Prunus virginiana *Rosaceae*
Plate 14, Nos. 1, 2 & 3

Description: Shrub 10-20 (sometimes 30) feet tall, trunk short, leaning, often crooked; branches spreading. Leaves 2-4 inches long, simple, alternate, egg-shaped and pointed at the tips, finely toothed, dull dark green above, paler on the lower surface. Flowers about ½ inch in diameter, with 5 rounded white petals arranged in many-flowered clusters 3-6 inches long, blooms in late May and June. Fruit occurs in drooping clusters; individual fruit ½ inch in diameter, nearly round, red, fleshy, astringent, maturing in July and August; containing a single round seed. Bark brown, becoming brown-gray and roughened with age. *Occurrence*: Thickets, open woods and abandoned fields. *Similar species*: The rum cherry (*P. serotina*) is larger, bears purplish black fruit, and has narrower leaves. *Comments*: Although the seeds are poisonous, the flesh of the fruit can be made into jelly. The raw fruit is very astringent, which accounts for its common name. A black fruited form, *P. virginiana* var. *melanocarpa*, occurs in the central Adirondacks.

AMERICAN MOUNTAIN ASH
Sorbus americana

ROSE FAMILY
Rosaceae
Plate 13, No. 3

Description: Small tree 10-15 (occasionally 20) feet tall, trunk short; branches nearly horizontal or ascending, spreading. Leaves 6-10 inches long, pinnately compound, alternate; leaflets 9-17, 2-3 inches long, thinly lance-shaped, tapering to a long point, finely and sharply toothed, bright green above, paler below, turning yellow in autumn. Flowers bloom in June in showy flat-topped clusters 4-5 inches in diameter; individual flowers white, ⅛ - ¼ inch in diameter, with 5 rounded petals. Fruit berry-like, about ¼ inch in diameter, bright red, in showy clusters like the flowers; flesh yellow, with an ashy odor, enclosing 2-4 yellow, tear-shaped seeds; maturing in September and October, some persisting. Bark grayish brown to reddish brown, smooth, becoming rough with age. *Occurrence*: Moist or rocky hillsides, mountain slopes, and stream banks. *Similar species*: The shrubby mountain ash (*S. decora*) has shorter, broader leaflets that are smooth on the undersurface. Its fruit is more orange, ⅜ inch in diameter, with 1-2 thin brown seeds, and is found mainly in September. The rowan tree (*S. aucupari*), introduced from Europe, has fruit and foliage most similar to the shrubby mountain ash, except that the leaflets are somewhat hairy on the underside (use hand lens). *Comments*: Formerly known as *Pyrus americana.* Although edible, the fruit is far too acidic to be eaten raw. A few berries may be cooked with any meat dish to impart a slight smoked flavor.

APPLE ROSE FAMILY
Malus sylvestris *Rosaceae*
Plate 15, Nos. 3 & 4

Description: Tree 20-30 (occasionally 40) feet tall, trunk straight or somewhat crooked, stout; branches ascending and spreading. Leaves 2-4 inches long, simple, alternate, oval, wavy saw-toothed, smooth, dark green on the upper surface, paler and covered with grayish hairs below. Flowers 1 inch in diameter, white, tinged with pink, with 5 rounded petals, in small clusters, blooming in late May. Fruit an edible apple, 2-3½ inches in diameter, rounded, yellow, green, red, containing up to 10 seeds, ripe in September and October. Bark gray-brown, scaly. *Occurrence*: Widespread along roadsides, pastures, and cleared areas. *Similar species*: Wild pear (*Pyrus communis*) is a tree similar in outline, but its leaves have smaller or no teeth on the margins, and are less hairy beneath. The small fruit is characteristically tapered near the stem. It is hard and puckery when raw, but often delicious when cooked. *Comments*: Formerly known as *Pyrus malus*. This is the commonly cultivated apple that is often not recognized when growing wild. Introduced from Europe. Source of cider.

Sand Cherry
Prunus pumila, page 44

RED CHOKEBERRY ROSE FAMILY
Aronia arbutifolia *Rosaceae*
Plate 16, No. 1
Description: Shrub 3-8 (sometimes 12) feet tall, with slender and often clustered stems. Leaves simple, alternate, 1½-3 inches long, oval to oblong, tips usually pointed, margins finely sharp-toothed, olive green above, paler and downy beneath, turning scarlet to orange in autumn. Flowers bloom in May, in small clusters; individual flowers about ½ inch across, with 5 round, white petals. Fruit borne in small flat clusters; individual fruit about ¼ inch long, apple-like, red; flesh astringent, usually enclosing 2 seeds, maturing in September. Bark grayish brown. *Occurrence*: Moist thickets; also found in drier sandy soils. *Similiar species*: Black chokeberry (*A. melanocarpa*) has leaves which are smooth beneath, and purple-black fruit. *Comments*: The fruit is highly astringent and puckery, hence the common name of chokeberry.

BLACK CHOKEBERRY ROSE FAMILY
Aronia melanocarpa *Rosaceae*
Plate 16, No. 2
Description: Shrub 2-5 (sometimes 10) feet tall, with slender branching stems. Leaves simple, alternate, 2-2½ inches long, oblong, tips pointed, margin finely dull-toothed, dark green above, paler and smooth beneath. Flowers bloom in May, in small clusters; individual flowers about ½ inch across, with 5 round, white petals. Fruit borne in small flat clusters; individual fruit ¼-½ inch wide, almost round, dark purple to shining black; flesh purple, juicy, edible, somewhat astringent, enclosing 2-4 oval, yellow-brown seeds, maturing in August. Bark grayish, smooth. *Occurrence*: Variable, ranging from swamps and moist ground to rocky uplands. *Similar species*: Red chokeberry (*A. arbutifolia*) has leaves which are downy beneath, and red fruit. *Comments*: Was *Pyrus melanocarpa* and *A. nigra*.

BROAD-LEAVED MEADOWSWEET ROSE FAMILY
Spirea latifolia *Rosaceae*
Plate 16, No. 4

Description: An upright shrub 2-5 feet tall, frequently forming thickets and hedges along moist ground. Leaves simple, alternate, 2-4 inches long, oblong, coarsely and unevenly toothed, tips blunt, light green above, paler beneath. Flowers bloom in July, in broadly based upright clusters 3-5 inches high; individual flowers white, with five round petals, ¼-⅓ inch broad. Fruit numerous dry capsules in upright clusters 3-5 inches high, maturing in autumn. Bark reddish brown, smooth. *Occurrence*: Damp open swamps and roadsides. *Similar species*: Narrow-leaved meadowsweet (*S. alba*) differs in having thinner, lance-shaped leaves that are more finely toothed and pointed at the tip. The flower clusters are not as broad at the base. *Comments*: Very common throughout the Adirondacks; found in practically every wet area.

HARDHACK ROSE FAMILY
Spirea tomentosa *Rosaceae*
Plate 17, No. 1

Description: An upright shrub 2-4 feet tall, usually growing in small clusters. Leaves simple, alternate, 1-3 inches long, oval to oblong, coarsely and unevenly toothed, dark green above, white to brown and downy beneath. Flowers in July, in upright clusters 3-5 inches high; individual flowers rosy pink, with five round petals, about ⅓ inch broad. Fruit numerous, dry, woody capsules in upright clusters 3-5 inches high, maturing in autumn. Bark brownish, wooly along the upper stem. *Occurrence*: Swamps and open moist ground. *Similar species*: The outline of the leaves resembles the broad-leaved meadowsweet (*S. latifolia*), but its undersides are not downy, and its upper stem is not wooly. *Comments*: Also known as steeplebush.

PLATE 1

1. *Taxus canadensis* — Page 16

2. *Abies balsamea* — Page 16

3. *Tsuga canadensis* — Page 17

4. *Pinus banksiana* — Page 17

PLATE 2

1. *Pinus resinosa* Page 18

2. *Pinus rigida* Page 18

3. *Pinus strobus* Page 19

4. *Pinus sylvestris* Page 19

PLATE 3

1. *Larix laricina*   Page 20

2. *Thuja occidentalis*   Page 20

3. *Juniperus communis* var. *depressa*
Page 21

4. *Juniperus virginiana*   Page 21

PLATE 4

1. *Picea rubens* — Page 22

2. *Picea mariana* — Page 22

3. *Picea glauca* — Page 22

4. *Picea abies* — Page 22

PLATE 5

1. *Populus balsamifera*   Page 24   2. *Populus deltoides*   Page 24

3. *Populus grandidentata*   Page 25   4. *Populus tremuloides*   Page 25

PLATE 6

1. *Salix discolor* — Page 27

2. *Salix caprea* — Page 27

3. *Salix alba* — Page 26

4. *Salix fragilis* — Page 26

PLATE 7

1. *Carya ovata* — Page 29

2. *Carya glabra* — Page 28

3. *Juglans cinerea* — Page 29

4. *Juglans nigra* — Page 29

PLATE 8

1. *Alnus rugosa* Page 30

2. *Alnus glutinosa* Page 30

3. *Betula papyrifera* var. *cordifolia*
Page 31

4. *Betula alleghaniensis* Page 30

1. *Ostraya virginiana* Page 33

2. *Carpinus caroliniana* Page 33

3. *Corylus americana* Page 32

4. *Corylus cornuta* Page 32

PLATE 10

1. *Castanea dentata* Page 34

2. *Fagus grandifolia* Page 35

3. *Quercus rubra* Page 37

4. *Quercus velutina* Page 37

1. *Quercus alba* — Page 36

2. *Quercus bicolor* — Page 36

3. *Quercus prinus* — Page 36

4. *Ulmus americana* — Page 39

PLATE 12

1. *Ulmus rubra* — Page 39

2. *Celtis occidentalis* — Page 38

3. *Ribes triste* — Page 40-41

4. *Ribes lacustre* — Page 40-41

PLATE 13

1. *Amelanchier* sp.   Page 42

2. *Amelanchier laevis*   Page 42

3. *Sorbus americana*   Page 46

4. *Sorbus decora*   Page 46

PLATE 14

1. *Prunus virginiana* — Page 45

2. *Prunus virginiana* — Page 45

3. *Prunus virginiana* var. *melanocarpa*
Page 45

4. *Prunus serotina* — Page 45

PLATE 15

1. *Crateagus* sp. Page 43

2. *Pyrus communis* Page 47

3. *Malus sylvestris* Page 47

4. *Malus sylvestris* Page 47

PLATE 16

1. *Aronia arbutifolia*   Page 48

2. *Aronia melanocarpa*   Page 48

3. *Spirea alba*   Page 49

4. *Spirea latifolia*   Page 49

PLATE 17

1. *Spirea tomentosa* — Page 49

2. *Rosa multiflora* — Page 89

3. *Rosa carolina* — Page 88

4. *Rosa palustris* — Page 89

PLATE 18

1. *Rosa acicularis*   Page 88
2. *Rosa acicularis*   Page 88

3. *Physocarpus opulifolius*   Page 85
4. *Physocarpus opulifolius*   Page 85

PLATE 19

1. *Rubus idaeus*   Page 87

2. *Rubus alleghaniensis*   Page 86

3. *Rubus odoratus*   Page 85

4. *Rubus odoratus*   Page 85

PLATE 20

1. *Rhus typhina* — Page 90

2. *Rhus typhina* — Page 90

3. *Acer spicatum* — Page 92

4. *Acer pensylvanicum* — Page 90

PLATE 21

1. *Acer saccharum* — Page 92

2. *Acer platanoides* — Page 92

3. *Acer nigrum* — Page 92

4. *Acer saccharinum* — Page 91

PLATE 22

1. *Acer rubrum* — Page 91

2. *Acer rubrum* — Page 91

3. Top to bottom: *Acer saccharinum, saccharum, platanoides* — Page 91-92

4. Top to bottom: *Acer pensylvanicum, rubrum, spicatum* — Page 90-92

PLATE 23

1. *Cornus alternifolia*   Page 93

2. *Cornus alternifolia*   Page 93

3. *Cornus obliqua*   Page 93

4. *Cornus racemosa*   Page 94

PLATE 24

1. *Cornus rugosa*   Page 94

2. *Cornus stolonifera*   Page 95

3. Left to right: *Ledum groenlandicum, Andromeda glaucophylla*   Page 96

4. *Kalmia latifolia*   Page 98

PLATE 25

1. *Kalmia augustifolia*   Page 97

2. *Kalmia polifolia*   Page 97

3. *Rhododendron maximum*   Page 98

4. Ornamental *Rhododendron*   Page 98

PLATE 26

1. *Rhododendron roseum* Page 99

2. *Exobasidium rhododendri* on Azalea
Page 99

3. *Rhododendron canadense* Page 99

4. *Vaccinium myrtilloides* Page 100

PLATE 27

1. *Gaylussacia baccata*   Page 101

2. *Gaylussacia baccata*   Page 101

3. *Vaccinium stamineum*   Page 101

4. *Vaccinium stamineum*   Page 101

PLATE 28

1. *Sambucus pubens* Page 105

2. *Sambucus pubens* Page 105

3. *Sambucus canadensis* Page 105

4. *Sambucus canadensis* Page 105

PLATE 29

1. *Fraxinus americana* — Page 102

2. *Diervilla lonicera* — Page 102

3. *Lonicera canadensis* — Page 103

4. *Lonicera canadensis* — Page 103

PLATE 30

1. *Lonicera bella* — Page 103

2. *Lonicera bella* — Page 103

3. *Symphoricarpos racemosus* — Page 106

4. *Viburnum acerifolium* — Page 106

PLATE 31

1. *Viburnum recognitum*   Page 109

2. *Viburnum recognitum*   Page 109

3. *Viburnum trilobum*   Page 109

4. *Viburnum trilobum*   Page 109

PLATE 32

1. *Viburnum lentago*   Page 108

2. *Viburnum lentago*   Page 108

3. *Viburnum cassinoides*   Page 108

4. *Viburnum alnifolium*   Page 107

PLATE 33

1. *Daphne mezereum*   Page 110

2. *Ilex verticillata*   Page 111

3. *Myrica gale*   Page 111

4. *Rhamnus cathartica*   Page 114

PLATE 34

1. *Nemopanthus mucronata*   Page 112

2. *Comptonia peregrina*   Page 112

3. *Berberis vulgaris*   Page 113

4. *Hamamelis virginiana*   Page 113

PLATE 35

1. *Cephalanthus occidentalis* Page 115

2. *Staphylea trifolia* Page 115

3. *Aralia hispida* Page 116

4. *Aralia racemosa* Page 116

PURPLE-FLOWERING RASPBERRY   ROSE FAMILY
Rubus odoratus   *Rosaceae*
Plate 19, Nos. 3 & 4

Description: Spreading shrub 3-5 feet high, often forming clusters or thickets. Leaves simple, alternate, broad, maple-like, 3 to 5 lobed, lobes pointed, margins irregularly toothed, bright green above, paler beneath. Flowers bloom in July, in small open clusters; individual flowers showy, rose-like, 1-2 inches across, with 5 broad petals, pink to light purple. Fruit berry-like, dull red, cup-shaped, separating easily from the core, finely hairy, juicy, acid and insipid to taste, maturing in August. Bark yellow-brown, separating into strips, upper limbs heavily covered with purplish hairs. *Occurrence*: Found along the margins of woods, streams and trails. *Similar species*: Our native wild roses have similar flowers, but they have compound leaves and usually sharply thorned stems. *Comments*: Often called thimbleberry, but this name is best reserved for a similar but white flowering species found in Canada and the western United States.

NINE-BARK   ROSE FAMILY
Physocarpus opulifolius   *Rosaceae*
Plate 18, Nos. 3 & 4

Description: Shrub 4-10 feet tall, usually with a single main stem supporting many ascending branches. Leaves simple, alternate, 1-3½ inches long, broad, maple-like, 3-lobed, margin irregularly round-toothed, dark green above, paler beneath. Flowers bloom in late May, in many showy clusters 1½-2 inches across, clusters nearly spherical; individual flowers white, about ¼ inch wide, with 5 rounded petals. Fruit a circular cluster of 20-24 inflated pods, cluster 2 inches across, first light red, maturing to pale brown; each pod 3-chambered, about ³/₈ inch long, each chamber housing a single tear-shaped yellow-brown seed, maturing in September. Bark light brown, peeling off in strips. *Occurrence*: Found in moist habitats, along stream banks and low swampy ground. *Similar species*: When in bloom, this shrub may easily be mistaken for a hawthorn (*Crataegus*), but it lacks the long thorns characteristic of the hawthorn family. *Comments*: The seed pods are distinctly rosy when first forming, and may be mistaken at first glance for small pink flowers.

COMMON BLACKBERRY
Rubus allegh006eniensis

ROSE FAMILY
Rosaceae
Plate 19, No. 2

Description: Shrub 3-6 feet high, with several spreading, arching stems, armed with both thorns and hair-like prickles. Leaves palmately compound, alternate, 3-10 inches long; leaflets 5 on the lower stem, 3 on the upper stem; leaflets broadly lance-shaped with a tapering point, margins double-toothed, deep green above, paler and velvety beneath. Flowers bloom in June, several in an open cluster; individual flowers about ½ inch wide, white, with 5 petals. Fruit berry-like, black, globular, about ¾ inch long, not separating easily from the core, flesh rather dry, edible, maturing August and September. Stems vertically ridged, dark red to purplish. *Occurrence*: Open fields, along woodland trails, roadsides. *Similar species*: The smooth blackberry (*R. canadensis*) also has ridged stems and similarly shaped leaves, but the leaves are smooth beneath and more evenly toothed. The fruit is also larger and juicier. The common name refers to the absence or scarcity of thorns and prickles on this species. *Comments*: The fruit of all species of blackberries is sought out for making desserts and sweet liqueurs.

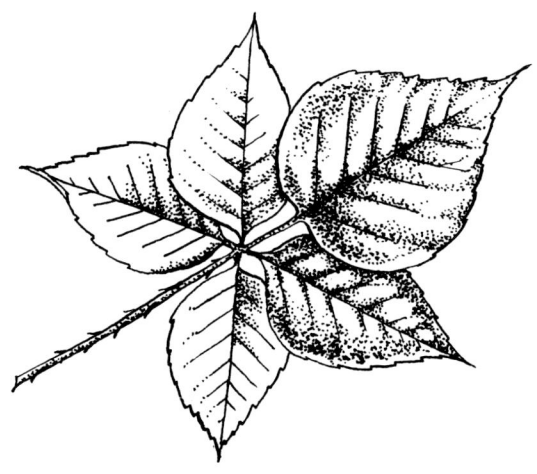

Common Blackberry Leaf
Rubus allegheniensis

RED RASPBERRY
Rubus idaeus
ROSE FAMILY
Rosaceae
Plate 19, No. 1

Description: Shrub 3-6 feet high, with several round, spreading, arching stems, armed with sharp hair-like prickles. Leaves pinnately compound, alternate, 3-10 inches long; leaflets 5 on lower stem, 3 on upper stem; leaflets oblong with a tapering point, margins coarsely and irregularly toothed, bright green above, pale green beneath, turning red in autumn. Flowers bloom in June, several in an open cluster; individual flowers about ½ inch wide, white, with 5 petals. Fruit berry-like, bright red, round, separating easily from the core, juicy, edible, maturing in July. Stems new growth round, mostly smooth, very pale green, armed with hair-like prickles; older growth darker. *Occurrence*: Along woodland trails, edges of woods, recently disturbed soils. *Similar species*: The black raspberry (*R. occidentalis*) has similar leaves, but may be differentiated by the stem and the fruit. The lower stem is purple to maroon, and the upper stem is heavily protected by stout, hooked prickles. The fruit is red when unripe, becoming dark purple to almost black when mature. *Comments*: Previously listed as a variety of *R. strigosus*, the European red raspberry.

Red Raspberry Leaf
Rubus idaeus

PRICKLY ROSE
Rosa acicularis

ROSE FAMILY
Rosaceae
Plate 18, Nos. 1 & 2

Description: Shrub 2-3 feet tall, stalk stout and erect, heavily protected by many stiff prickles. Leaves pinnately compound, alternate, with 5-7 leaflets; leaflets sharply toothed, dark green above, paler beneath, turning red in autumn; stipules narrow at the base, widely flaring at the tips. Flowers bloom in mid-July, singly or in small clusters; individual flowers with 5 broad pink petals, center either solid yellow or yellow surrounding a small pink area, 2-2½ inches across, fragrant. Fruit a "hip," spherical, ¾ inch long, red; flesh dry, yellow, enclosing 5-20 yellow-brown seeds, maturing in early autumn, persisting. Bark reddish brown. *Occurrence*: On moist ground, the edge of woods, in rocky areas. *Similar species*: Despite its name, the smooth rose (*R. blanda*), may also have many hair-like prickles near the base of the stem. It may be differentiated by the absence of spines on the upper branches, smaller fruit, and stipules which are wide but not as flaring. *Comments*: One of the Adirondacks' largest flowering wild roses.

PASTURE ROSE
Rosa carolina

ROSE FAMILY
Rosaceae
Plate 17, No. 2

Description: Shrub 1-3 feet high with spreading stems armed with slender, straight thorns. Leaves pinnately compound, alternate, usually 5 leaflets, with toothed margins, dark green above, paler beneath, turning bright red to orange in fall; stipules narrow. Flowers bloom in late June through early July, solitary to small clusters; individual flowers with five broad pink petals, yellow center, fragrant. Fruit a "hip," spherical, red; flesh dry, yellow, enclosing numerous round seeds, maturing in early autumn, persisting. Bark brownish, smooth with occasional thorns. *Occurrence*: Found on dry, sunny soils. *Similar species*: The combination of short size, straight thorns and dry habitat separate this rose from all others. *Comments*: The earliest blooming of our wild pink-flowering roses. Was *Rosa humilis*.

SWAMP ROSE *Rosa palustris*

ROSE FAMILY
Rosaceae
Plate 17, No. 4

Description: Shrub 2-7 feet tall, with erect to spreading stems protected by stout, hooked thorns. Leaves pinnately compound, alternate, usually 7 (sometimes 5 or 9) leaflets, margins very finely toothed, dark green above, paler beneath, turning red to orange in autumn; stipules long and narrow. Flowers bloom in late July, in clusters; individual flowers with five broad pink petals, yellow centers, about 2 inches across, fragrant. Fruit a "hip," occurring in clusters; individual fruit spherical, 3/8 - 1/2 inch in diameter, red; flesh dry, yellow, enclosing 15-40 small yellow seeds, maturing in early autumn, persisting. Bark brown, armed with both thorns and prickles. *Occurrence*: Swamps, low moist ground, and stream borders. *Similar species*: The height, stout thorns and wet habitat combination separate this rose from *R. blanda* and *R. carolina*. *Comments*: In older texts this description would be found under *R. carolina*, a name now reserved for a smaller species.

MULTIFLORA ROSE *Rosa multiflora*

ROSE FAMILY
Rosaceae
Plate 17, No. 2

Description: Shrub 5-10 feet tall with many widely spreading stems up to 10 feet long, well armed with stout curved thorns. Leaves pinnately compound, alternate, with 7 to usually 9 leaflets, margins sharply toothed, bright green above, paler beneath, becoming purple in autumn; stipules heavily fringed. Flowers bloom in mid-June, in numerous and crowded clusters; individual flowers ¾ inch across, with five white petals, barely fragrant. Fruit a "hip," spherical, usually less than ¼ inch in diameter, dull red, many in a cluster, flesh thin, enclosing 4-5 cylindrical seeds, maturing in early autumn, persisting. Bark brown. *Occurrence*: Old pastures, roadsides. *Similar species*: The large size, numerous white flowers and spreading nature differentiate this rose from all others. *Comments*: An intentional import from Asia. Once escaped, it quickly forms impenetrable thickets, endangering pastures and crowding out native plants.

STAGHORN SUMAC
Rhus typhina

CASHEW FAMILY
Anacardiaceae
Plate 20, Nos. 1 & 2

Description: Small tree 10-20 (occasionally 30) feet tall, trunk short, dividing to form ascending branches; branch tips covered with velvety hairs; typically forming dense thickets. Leaves 16-24 inches long, pinnately compound, alternate; leaflets 11-31, oblong, tips pointed, sharply toothed, dark green above, paler beneath, becoming scarlet in autumn. Flowers yellowish green, small, growing in dense, upright, conical clusters 8-12 inches tall, blooming early July. Fruit borne in velvety, maroon, upright, conical clusters 8-12 inches long; seeds round, covered with velvety red hairs, seed coating pleasantly acidic, lemon-like in taste, ripening in late August, often persisting. Bark brown or brown-gray. *Occurrence*: Dry soil along roadsides and in young woodlots. *Similar species*: None. *Comments*: Named for its winter silhouette which resembles the antlers of the European red stag. A refreshing pink lemonade-like drink can be made from the red fruit by stirring whole clusters in cold water, straining through cloth, and adding sugar to taste.

STRIPED MAPLE
Acer pensylvanicum

MAPLE FAMILY
Aceraceae
Plate 20, No. 4; Plate 22, No. 4

Description: A shrub or small tree 10-20 (sometimes 30) feet high, with a slender trunk and few ascending branches. Leaves simple, opposite, 4-6 inches long, 3-lobed, the tips thin and pointed, margins finely and sharply toothed, dark green above, light green beneath. Flowers bloom in late May and early June, yellowish green, several along a drooping stalk. Fruit paired, winged keys attached by thin stalks, hanging in clusters; individual keys about 1 inch long, green, maturing in late summer. Bark smooth, light green, vertically striped with white to ruddy brown markings. *Occurrence*: Common on rich hillsides. *Similar species*: No other species exhibits such distinctively striped bark. *Comments*: Also called goosefoot, in reference to the outline of the leaf.

RED MAPLE MAPLE FAMILY
Acer rubrum *Aceraceae*
Plate 22, Nos. 1, 2 & 4

Description: Tree 30-60 (sometimes 75) feet tall, symmetrical in outline, with heavy ascending branches. Leaves simple, opposite, 2½-4½ inches long, 3 (rarely 5) lobed, lobes taper-pointed, margins coarsely toothed, dark green above, whitish green beneath, turning bright red in autumn; stalk long, bright red above. Flowers bloom in April before the leaves appear, in small clusters, scarlet. Fruit paired, winged keys attached by long thin stalks, in drooping clusters; individual keys ¾-1 inch long, red, maturing in June. Bark gray, smooth when young, darkening and becoming furrowed. *Occurrence*: Common in any moist, wooded area. *Similar species*: Silver maple (*A. saccharinum*) also blooms at the same time, but the two can be differentiated by bruising the bark of young twigs. Those of the silver maple smell offensive, those of the red maple do not. *Comments*: True to its name, the red maple turns scarlet twice each year; first when flowering and again in the fall when the leaves brighten.

SILVER MAPLE MAPLE FAMILY
Acer saccharinum *Aceraceae*
Plate 21, No. 4; Plate 22, No. 3

Description: Tree 40-60 (sometimes 90) feet high, with heavy spreading limbs often drooping at the tips. Leaves simple, opposite, 3-6 inches long, with five deeply cut lobes, the lobes sharply and irregularly toothed, bright green above, silvery green beneath, turning yellow in autumn. Flowers bloom in April before the leaves unfold, in crowded clusters; individual flowers small, yellow-green. Fruit paired, winged keys attached by long thin stalks, in drooping clusters; individual keys 2-3 inches long, straw colored when mature, dropping in August. Bark dark gray, scaly. *Occurrence*: Along river banks and in lowland woods. *Similar species*: Red maple (*A. rubrum*) blooms at the same time, but the two can be differentiated by bruising the twigs. Those of the silver maple smell offensive; twigs of the red maple do not. *Comments*: Also known as the soft maple, white maple, river maple, water maple and swamp maple. Was *A. dasycarpum*.

SUGAR MAPLE MAPLE FAMILY
Acer saccharum *Aceraceae*
Plate 21, No. 1; Plate 22, No. 3

Description: Tree 50-80 (occasionally 100 or more) feet tall, very symmetrical, trunk straight, major branches ascending. Leaves simple, opposite, 3-5½ inches in diameter, with 3 to usually 5 lobe-like divisions, margins with a few large teeth, dark green above, paler green below, turning yellow, orange or red in autumn; very long-stemmed. Flowers bloom in May, in drooping long-stemmed clusters; individual flowers small, greenish yellow. Fruit paired, winged keys attached by long thin stalks, in drooping clusters; individual keys 1-1¾ inches long, maturing in September and October. Bark dark gray, furrowed. *Occurrence*: Common in rich woods and on rocky hillsides. *Similar species*: Norway maple (*A. platanoides*), often planted as an ornamental, has identical leaves but milky sap in the leaf stems (those in the sugar maple have clear sap), flower in round bright green clusters and have larger, flat, widely spread keys. Black maple (*A. nigrum*), which some believe to be only a variety or subspecies of sugar maple, has identical keys but broader, barely toothed leaves with typically drooping margins. *Comments*: Also known as rock maple and hard maple. State tree of New York. Best source of maple syrup and sugar.

MOUNTAIN MAPLE MAPLE FAMILY
Acer spicatum *Aceraceae*
Plate 20, No. 3; Plate 22, No. 4

Description: Shrub or small tree 10-20 (sometimes 30) feet tall, with a slender trunk and ascending branches. Leaves simple, opposite, 3-5 inches long, 3 (occasionally 5) lobed, lobes pointed, margins coarsely toothed, dull green above, lighter beneath, turning reddish orange in autumn. Flowers bloom in late May and June, in upright spike-like clusters; individual flowers small, greenish yellow. Fruit paired, winged keys attached by thin stalks, in drooping clusters; individual keys about ¾ inch long, pink tinged, maturing in late summer. Bark brown-gray, slightly rough. *Occurrence*: Common in shaded woodlands, roadsides. *Similar species*: Striped maple (*A. pensylvanicum*) has similar leaves and is of similar size, but has smooth green bark with vertical stripes.

GREEN OISER DOGWOOD
Cornus alternifolia

DOGWOOD FAMILY
Cornaceae
Plate 23, Nos. 1 & 2

Description: Shrub or small tree 6-25 feet high, with a single, erect trunk and alternating branches. Leaves simple, mostly in clusters at the end of the branches, 2-4 inches long, oval, tips extended and pointed, margins usually smooth, lustrous green above, whitish green beneath, turning yellow to scarlet in autumn. Flowers bloom in late June, in erect flat-topped clusters 1½-2½ inches across; individual flowers small, white, 4-petaled. Fruit borne in flat-topped, crimson-stemmed clusters 2½-3½ inches across; individual fruit round, about ⅓ inch in diameter, leaden blue; flesh pinkish, thin, enclosing a single irregularly shaped stone, maturing in August or September. Bark variable, from bright green to reddish tinged to brown. *Occurrence*: Stream banks, rich wooded soils and roadsides. *Similar species*: No other Adirondack dogwood reaches tree size. *Comments*: The common name refers to the striking green color usually exhibited by the branches. This is the tallest of all Adirondack dogwoods.

BLUE COLONEL
Cornus obliqua

DOGWOOD FAMILY
Cornaceae
Plate 23, No. 3

Description: Shrub 3-8 feet tall with spreading branches. Leaves simple, opposite, 3-5 inches long, oval, tips pointed, margins smooth, bright green above, pale green beneath, turning red to purple in autumn. Flowers bloom in mid-June, in rounded clusters 1½-2½ inches wide; individual flowers small, creamy white, 4-petaled. Fruit borne in flat clusters; individual fruit globular, ¼ inch in diameter, pale to leaden blue; flesh whitish, bitter, enclosing a single irregularly round seed, maturing in September. Bark light brown. *Occurrence*: Along swamps and lakes, in moist soils. *Similar species*: The newer branches have a purplish coloration that mimics the red oiser dogwood (*C. stolonifera*), but this species may be differentiated by its smaller stature and white fruit. *Comments*: Also known as *C. amomum* ssp. *obliqua*. Other common names are the silky colonel and kinnikinnik.

GRAY-STEMMED DOGWOOD   DOGWOOD FAMILY
Cornus racemosa   *Cornaceae*
Plate 23, No. 4

Description: Shrub 4-10 feet high, with numerous ascending stems and branches that often form inpenetrable dome-shaped thickets and clusters. Leaves simple, opposite, 2½-4 inches long, lance-shaped, tips pointed, margins smooth, olive green above, paler beneath. Flowers bloom in mid-June, in clusters 1½-2 inches across; individual flowers small, creamy white, 4-petaled. Fruit borne in flat-topped, light crimson-stemmed clusters; individual fruit globular, almost ½ inch in diameter, greenish white; flesh thin, white, enclosing a single irregularly round stone, maturing in August or September, often persisting into early winter. Bark gray, smooth. *Occurrence*: In open fields and along moist areas. *Similar species*: Red oiser dogwood (*C. stolonifera*) also has white fruit, but may be differentiated by its wine red bark. *Comments*: Also known as *C. paniculata*.

ROUND-LEAVED DOGWOOD   DOGWOOD FAMILY
Cornus rugosa   *Cornaceae*
Plate 24, No. 1

Description: Shrub 3-10 feet high, with a single or sometimes several trunks; branches spreading. Leaves simple, opposite, 2-6 inches long, broadly oval to almost round, tips pointed, margins smooth, pale green above, gray-green beneath. Flowers bloom in mid-June, in rounded clusters 1½-3 inches wide; individual flowers small, white, 4-petaled. Fruit borne in flat clusters; individual fruit globular, 3/8 inch in diameter, usually pale blue; flesh aromatic, bitter, enclosing a single ridged round seed, maturing in late August or September. Bark dark reddish purple. *Occurrence*: Wooded areas with sandy or rocky soil. *Similar species*: The reddish bark may lead to confusion with the red oiser dogwood (*C. stolonifera*), but that species has pure white fruit. *Comments*: The least known of our dogwoods. Was *C. circinata*.

RED OISER DOGWOOD   DOGWOOD FAMILY
Cornus stolonifera   *Cornaceae*
Plate 24, No. 2

Description: Shrub 3-6 feet high, with spreading, sometimes prostrate stems, forming low thickets. Leaves simple, opposite, 3-4 inches long, lance-shaped with a rounded base, tips taper-pointed, margins smooth, olive green above, whitish green beneath. Flowers bloom in early June, in small flat clusters 1½-2 inches across; individual flowers small, dull white, 4-petaled. Fruit borne in flat-topped, ruddy-stemmed clusters about 3 inches across; individual fruit globular, ¼-⅓ inch in diameter, white tipped with a black "eye"; flesh thin, white, enclosing a single irregularly shaped stone, maturing in August. Bark rich brown near the base, the outer or upper surfaces a bright maroon-red. *Occurrence*: Open moist soils, margins of wet areas and meadows. *Similar species*: Blue colonel (*C. obliqua*) sometimes has dark maroon branches, but this species may be differentiated by its downy twigs and blue fruit. *Comments*: Both the first and the last of our native dogwoods to flower. After the fruits mature in August, the red oiser often has a second blooming season.

CASSANDRA   HEATH FAMILY
Chamaedaphne calyculata   *Ericaceae*

Description: Shrub 2-4 feet high, often spreading to form dense thickets. Leaves simple, alternate, ½-1½ inches long, oblong, tips usually blunt, margins minutely toothed, leathery, dull green above, paler beneath. Flowers bloom in May, in small one-sided clusters; individual flowers white or with a pinkish tinge, cylindrical to urn-shaped, ¼ inch long. Fruit in small clusters like the flowers; individual fruit woody, globular, 5-sided, many-seeded, maturing in late summer, persisting. Bark dull brown. *Occurrence*: On bogs and along acid swamps. *Similar species*: None. *Comments:* A common but often overlooked resident of bogs and streambanks.

BOG ROSEMARY HEATH FAMILY
Andromeda glaucophylla *Ericaceae*
Plate 24, No. 3

Description: Shrub 1-3 feet high, with few branches, often lying almost prostrate. Leaves simple, alternate, 1-2 inches long, lance-shaped, tips pointed, margins smooth and usually rolled back, dark green above, downy white beneath. Flowers bloom in May and June, in few-flowered clusters; individual flowers globular, open at the tip, white tinged with pink, waxy, about ¼ inch long. Fruit a dry capsule, globular, 5-sided, woody, many-seeded, maturing in late summer. Bark brown to gray. *Occurrence*: Found mostly on acid bogs. *Similar species*: Labrador tea (*Ledum groenlandicum*) has larger, broader leaves and 5-petaled flowers. *Comments*: The common name stems from a visual resemblance to garden rosemary (*Rosmarinum officinalis*) of the mint family. Interestingly, although not closely related, there is also a resiny similarity in flavor. The latin name is a reference to Andromeda of ancient mythology. Like the plant, she was doomed to always have her feet submerged in water.

LABRADOR TEA HEATH FAMILY
Ledum groenlandicum *Ericaceae*
Plate 24, No. 3

Description: Shrub 1-4 feet high with several ascending stems, generally circular in outline. Leaves simple, alternate, 1-3 inches long, narrowly oblong, tips blunt, margins smooth and usually curled back, dark green above, white to rusty and wooly beneath, evergreen. Flowers bloom in June, in attractive globular clusters 1½-2½ inches across; individual flowers white, ½-¾ inch broad, with 5 rounded petals. Fruit occurring in clusters; individual fruit dry capsules, oval, ¼ inch long, brown, many seeded, maturing in late summer. Bark brown to grayish brown. *Occurrence*: On bogs, lake edges and moist shaded areas. *Similar species*: Bog rosemary (*Andromeda glaucophylla*) has smaller, thinner leaves and inflated, globular flowers. *Comments*: As the common name suggests, the leaves have been used to brew a somewhat bitter tea.

SHEEP LAUREL　　　　　　　　　　HEATH FAMILY
Kalmia augustifolia　　　　　　　　　　*Ericaceae*
　　　　　　　　　　　　　　　　　　Plate 25, No. 1

Description: Shrub 1-3 feet tall with rounded branches. Leaves simple, opposite or in whorls of 3, 1½-2½ inches long, broadly oval, tips blunt, margins smooth, deep green above, paler and smooth beneath, evergreen; stalk ¼-⅜ inch long. Flowers bloom in late June, in showy clusters along the stalk; individual flowers bowl-shaped with 5 shallow lobes, crimson red, ¼-½ inch across. Fruit a cluster of long-stemmed dry, woody, capsules; individual fruits circular, almost ¼ inch wide, enclosing many seeds, maturing in late summer, persisting. Bark brown to gray. *Occurrence*: Bogs, sandy pine forests, rocky soils. *Similar species*: Pale laurel (*K. polifolia*) has smaller, stalkless leaves. It has paler flowers, and blooms earlier in the season. *Comments*: Also known as lambkill, a reference to its (and all other laurels') poisonous foliage.

PALE LAUREL　　　　　　　　　　HEATH FAMILY
Kalmia polifolia　　　　　　　　　　　*Ericaceae*
　　　　　　　　　　　　　　　　　　Plate 25, No. 2

Description: Shrub 6-22 inches tall, with flattened 2-edged branches. Leaves simple, opposite or in whorls of 3, 1-1½ inches long, narrowly lance-shaped, tips usually blunt, margins smooth, dark green above, whitish and downy beneath, evergreen; leafstalks usually absent. Flowers bloom in early June, in rounded terminal clusters; individual flowers bowl-shaped with 5 shallow lobes, rich pink, ½-¾ inch across. Fruit a cluster of long-stemmed dry, woody capsules; individual fruit circular, almost ¼ inch wide, enclosing many seeds, maturing in late summer; persisting. Bark brown to black. *Occurrence*: Bogs and moist acid soils. *Similar species*: Sheep laurel (*K. augustifolia*) has broader, stalked leaves. It has redder flowers, and blooms later. *Comments*: Also known as the bog laurel, in reference to its preferred habitat.

MOUNTAIN LAUREL HEATH FAMILY
Kalmia latifolia *Ericaceae*
Plate 24, No. 4

Description: Shrub 3-6 (occasionally 20) feet tall, with irregularly spreading branches, sometimes forming dense thickets. Leaves simple, alternate, mostly crowded at the branch tips, 2-5 inches long, lance-shaped, tips pointed, margins smooth, shiny dark green above, paler beneath, evergreen. Flowers bloom in July, in dome-shaped terminal clusters 3-4 inches across; individual flowers bowl-shaped with 5 shallow lobes, white, sometimes tinged with pink, ¾-1 inch wide. Fruit a circular dry capsule, woody, small, reddish brown, enclosing many seeds, maturing in early autumn. Bark brown to reddish brown. *Occurrence*: Open woodlands; prefers steep slopes. *Similar species*: Great laurel (*Rhododendron maximum*) has similar but much larger leaves. Its flowers have rounded, petal-like lobes. *Comments*: Mountain laurel is probably native only to the eastern Adirondacks, but has been transplanted to the central region.

GREAT LAUREL HEATH FAMILY
Rhododendron maximum *Ericaceae*
Plate 25, No. 3

Description: Shrub or small tree 3-15 (occasionally 30) feet high, usually spreading and forming dense thickets. Leaves simple, alternate, 4-9 inches long, oblong to lance-shaped, tips pointed, margins smooth and often curled back, leathery, dark shiny green above, white to rusty and downy beneath, evergreen. Flowers bloom in July, in large and round terminal clusters; individual flowers with a short tubular base opening into 5 broad rounded lobes, ¾-1¼ inches across, white with a sprinkling of gold-green dots on the inner surface. Fruit a dry capsule, oblong, ½-1 inch long, woody, reddish brown, many seeded, maturing in early fall. Bark gray-brown. *Occurrence*: Shaded moist soils, especially lakeshores. *Similar species*: A domesticated cross (*R. maximum* X *canadense*) is frequently planted. It differs by having larger flowers with unequally lobed rose to orange blooms that flower in June. *R. maximum* is a rare plant deserving full protection from illicit diggings. *Comments*: Bees visiting these flowers produce poisonous honey.

WILD AZALEA HEATH FAMILY
Rhododendron roseum *Ericaceae*
Plate 26, Nos. 1 & 2

Description: Shrub 2-6 feet tall, with open branches and sparse foliage. Leaves simple, alternate, mostly in clusters at the branch tips, 2-4 inches long, tips pointed, margins smooth, yellow-green above, paler beneath, turning yellow in autumn. Flowers bloom in late May and June in small terminal clusters; individual flowers tubular with 5 widely flaring lobes, about 2 inches long, pale pink, extremely fragrant. Fruit a dry, woody capsule, oblong, erect, 1-1½ inches high, many seeded, maturing in autumn. Bark brown. *Occurrence*: Along streams, bogs and shaded moist woodlands. *Similar species*: Originally listed as *R. nudiflorum*, a name now reserved for a visually similar azalea differentiated by the flowers' lack of fragrance. *Comments*: During the flowering season, a fungal infection (*Exobasidium rhododendri*) swells some leaves into fruit-like structures popularly known as azalea apples. Previous authors reported eating these sweet and juicy "fruits," but this is not recommended because of the parent plant's documented toxicity.

RHODORA HEATH FAMILY
Rhododendron canadense *Ericaceae*
Plate 26, No. 3

Description: Shrub 1-3 feet high with thin spreading branches. Leaves simple, alternate, 1-2½ inches long, oblong to oval, tips blunt or bristle-tipped, margins smooth, light green above, paler beneath. Flowers bloom in terminal clusters, just as the leaves are emerging; individual flowers magenta, 1 inch long, honeysuckle-like, tubular but divided into 2 lips, the upper lip tipped with 3 short lobes, the lower lip deeply divided into 2 narrow lobes. Fruit a woody capsule, long and thin, having 5 divisions enclosing many seeds, maturing in autumn. Bark peeling, exposing a smooth, copper-colored inner surface. *Occurrence*: Bogs, stream banks and moist woodlands. *Similar species*: The flower could be confused with that of the fly honeysuckles (*Lonicera sp.*), but these have opposite leaves and fleshy, berry-like fruit. *Comments*: Rhodora was reliably reported as inhabiting Adirondack bogs at the turn of the century, but we failed to discover any existing populations.

HIGHBUSH BLUEBERRY
Vaccinium corymbosum

HEATH FAMILY
Ericaceae
Plate 26, No. 4

Description: Shrub 5-10 (sometimes 15) feet tall, with spreading branches, often forming large clumps. Leaves simple, alternate, 1½-3 inches long, oblong to oval, tips pointed, margins smooth, light green above, paler beneath, turning orange to scarlet in autumn. Flowers bloom late May to early June, in small terminal clusters; individual flowers white, sometimes pink-tinged, cylindrical to bell-shaped, 5-lobed at opening, ¼-½ inch long, waxy. Fruit borne in small terminal clusters; individual fruit round, ¼-⅓ inch in diameter, typically blue with a bloom; flesh juicy, edible, pleasantly acid, enclosing many tiny seeds, maturing in August. Bark gray to brown, rough and shredding. *Occurrence*: In swamps and all moist areas. *Similar species*: Low blueberry (*V. angustifolium*) is our shortest blueberry. It forms low mats, often under 1 foot in height, from lakeshores to the High Peaks. Velvet-leaf blueberry (*V. myrtilloides*) shares the habitat and appearance of the highbush blueberry, except that it is not quite as tall, and has velvety hairs along the young stems and on the undersides and margins of the leaves. The dryland blueberry (*V. pallidum*) generally grows less than 3 feet tall. Its habitat differs from other blueberries by living in dry, sandy ground. *Comments*: The fruit of Adirondack wild blueberries is eagerly sought out by berry pickers.

Highbush Blueberry
Vaccinum corymbosum

DEERBERRY
Vaccinium stamineum

HEATH FAMILY
Ericaceae
Plate 27, Nos. 3 & 4

Description: Shrub 2-6 feet tall, with widely spreading branches. Leaves simple, alternate, 1-3 inches long, oval, margins smooth, pale green above, whitish beneath. Flowers bloom in June, in terminal one-sided clusters; individual flowers yellowish green, tubular with 5 pointed and widely flaring lobes, about ¼ inch long. Fruit borne in sparse clusters; individual fruit round, about ½ inch in diameter, dull yellow-green, sometimes turning very light purple upon ripening; flesh juicy, edible, mildly sour, enclosing up to 20 flat brown seeds, maturing in September and October. Bark light brown. *Occurrence*: In dry woods and forested hillsides. *Similar species*: The blueberries have similarly shaped leaves and fruit, but much darker and sweeter fruit. *Comments*: Often found as an understory plant beneath white birch.

BLACK HUCKLEBERRY
Gaylussacia baccata

HEATH FAMILY
Ericaceae
Plate 27, Nos. 1 & 2

Description: Shrub 1-3 feet high with many erect branches. Leaves 1-2 inches long, simple, alternate, oblong to lance-shaped, tips pointed or rounded, edges smooth, green above, under surface paler and covered with tiny yellow resinous dots, turning red to purplish in autumn. Flowers in June, on short one-sided clusters; individual flowers tubular, cylindrical to bell-shaped, about ¼ inch long, dull red. Fruit a black or purplish berry-like drupe, about ¼ inch in diameter, round, sweet, edible, with ten yellow seeds, maturing in August. Bark dark gray, becoming darker with age, and peeling. *Occurrence*: On acid soils in rocky woods, thickets and bogs. *Similar species*: The blueberries (*Vaccinium sp.*) appear very similar, but usually have white to pink-tinged flowers, a whitish bloom on the fruit, and smaller seeds. *Comments*: When growing with blueberries, the fruit of the two is often mixed by pickers. Fortunately, both are equally edible. Was *G. resinosa*.

WHITE ASH
Fraxinus americana

OLIVE FAMILY
Oleaceae
Plate 29, No. 1

Description: Tree 50-75 (sometimes 80 or more) feet tall, trunk tall, straight, free of branches for several feet from the ground; branches horizontal to ascending and spreading. Leaves 8-12 inches long, pinnately compound, opposite; leaflets 7-9 (usually 7), 2-5 inches long, short-stalked, lance-shaped, edges smooth or finely toothed, dark green above, paler beneath, turning yellow to purple in early autumn. Flowers bloom in May before the leaves emerge, in small reddish purple clusters. Fruit 1-2 inches long, thin, tips blunt, long-winged, in drooping clusters about 7 inches long, maturing in late summer, persisting. Bark grayish brown. *Occurrence*: Common in hardwood forests. *Similar species*: Black ash (*F. nigra*) has stalkless, finely toothed leaflets. The winged seeds have a notched tip. Usually found near water. *Comments*: Common source of hardwood for sports equipment such as baseball bats and hockey sticks. One of the last trees to set leaves in the spring.

BUSH HONEYSUCKLE
Diervilla lonicera

HONEYSUCKLE FAMILY
Caprifoliaceae
Plate 29, No. 2

Description: Shrub 2-4 feet high, often with barely ascending branches running close to the ground. Leaves simple, opposite, 2-5 inches long, lance-shaped, tips extended and pointed, margins finely toothed, dark green above, paler beneath. Flowers bloom in July, in small terminal clusters; individual flowers about ¾ inch long, honey yellow, tubular with 5 recurving lobes. Fruit a dry, woody capsule, about ¾ inch long, slender, brown, 2-valved, many seeded, maturing in September. Bark brown to grayish brown. *Occurrence*: Wooded hillsides, frequently on rocky soils. *Similar species*: Often found growing near the early fly honeysuckle. (*Lonicera canadensis*), but this species has toothless leaves and juicy, red berries. *Comments*: The Adirondacks' only honeysuckle to fruit by means of a dry, woody capsule.

COMMON HONEYSUCKLE   HONEYSUCKLE FAMILY
Lonicera bella   *Caprifoliaceae*
Plate 30, Nos. 1 & 2

Description: Shrub 4-9 feet tall, frequently as wide as it is tall; branches spreading, usually ascending but with drooping tips. Leaves simple, opposite, 1-3 inches long, oval to oblong, tips rounded or minutely pointed, margins smooth, dark green above, paler beneath. Flowers bloom in June, in pairs; individual flowers tubular, irregularly 5-lobed, about ¾ inch long, pink to yellow, rarely white, usually not fragrant; flowerstalks ¾ inch or longer. Fruit paired berries, round, almost ½ inch wide, transluscent red or occasionally orange; flesh scarlet, very juicy, enclosing 2-6 red disc-shaped seeds, maturing in August. Bark gray to grayish brown. *Occurrence*: Roadsides and scrub areas bordering human habitation. *Similar species*: Tartarian honeysuckle (*L. tartarica*) has pink, or occasionally white, fragrant flowers. Morrow's honeysuckle (*L. morrowi*) is a smaller shrub with white to yellow flowers, borne on flowerstalks mostly under ¾ inch long. *Comments*: *L. bella* is a naturally occurring cross between *L. tartarica* and *L. morrowi*. *L. bella* has now emerged as the dominant species, and it has become difficult to find pure specimens of either *L. tartarica* or *L. morrowi*. Both of the parent species were introduced from Eurasia.

**EARLY FLY
HONEYSUCKLE**   HONEYSUCKLE FAMILY
Lonicera canadensis   *Caprifoliaceae*
Plate 29, Nos. 3 & 4

Description: Shrub 3-5 feet tall, with sparse and irregularly placed branches. Leaves simple, opposite, 1-2 inches long, oval to broadly oval, tips usually pointed, margins smooth, light green on both sides. Flowers bloom in May or early June, in pairs; individual flowers funnel-shaped, with 5 nearly equal lobes, ¾ inch long, yellow to greenish yellow. Fruit paired berries, egg-shaped, ¼ inch long, deep red; flesh juicy, enclosing several seeds, maturing in July. Bark gray to brownish gray. *Occurrence*: Established hardwoods. *Similar species*: Often found growing near the bush honeysuckle (*Diervilla lonicera*), but this species has toothed leaves and woody fruit. *Comments*: This is the first honeysuckle to bloom each year.

SWAMP FLY HONEYSUCKLE
Lonicera oblongifolia

HONEYSUCKLE FAMILY
Caprifoliaceae

Description: Shrub 2-5 feet high, with ascending branches. Leaves simple, opposite, 1-2 inches long, oblong to oval, tips rounded or minutely pointed, margins smooth, dark green above, gray-green beneath. Flowers bloom in June, in pairs; individual flowers ½ inch long, pale yellow outside, often marked with purple inside, tubular and deeply divided into 2 lips; upper lip 4-lobed, lower lip single lobed. Fruit paired berries, either distinct or united at the base, round, ¼-½ inch wide, crimson to purple-red; flesh juicy, enclosing several seeds, maturing in late summer. Bark gray to light brown. *Occurrence*: Found along bogs, wet woodlands and arbor vitae swamps. *Similar species*: In all stages except flowering, the swamp fly honeysuckle could be mistaken for a short common honeysuckle (*L. bella*), but the two do not share the same habitats. The common honeysuckle is found near human habitations. The swamp fly honeysuckle occurs in remote swamps. *Comments*: The azalea-like flowers are the showiest of Adirondack wild honeysuckles.

MOUNTAIN FLY HONEYSUCKLE
Lonicera villosa

HONEYSUCKLE FAMILY
Caprifoliaceae

Description: Shrub 1-3 feet high with erect branches. Leaves simple, opposite, 1-2½ inches long, oval to oblong, tips rounded, margins smooth, light green above, paler beneath. Flowers bloom in June, in pairs; individual flowers ½-¾ inch long, pale yellow, tubular with 5 nearly equal lobes. Fruit a single oblong berry, about ½ inch long, dark blue to bluish black with a bloom; flesh juicy, edible but often bitter, enclosing several seeds, ripening in July or August. Bark brown, shredding. *Occurrence*: Found along bogs and other wet areas, especially at higher altitudes. *Similar species*: The combination of blue fruit and high, swampy habitats separates this species from all other honeysuckles. *Comments*: The single fruit is formed by the united growths of both flowers. Because of this, the fruit has the unusual feature of sporting 2 "eyes" on the lower surface.

BLUE ELDERBERRY HONEYSUCKLE FAMILY
Sambucus canadensis *Caprifoliaceae*
Plate 28, Nos. 3 & 4

Description: Shrub 3-10 feet tall, often as wide as it is tall. Leaves compound, opposite, with 5-11 (typically 7) leaflets; individual leaflets lance-shaped, 3-6 inches long, edges finely toothed, tips sharp-pointed, dark green above, paler beneath. Flowers bloom in July, in showy flat-topped clusters, each cluster typically branched into 5 stems; individual flowers cream-white, about $1/5$ inch in diameter, fragrant. Fruit many in usually drooping flat-topped clusters 6-8 inches across; individual fruit round, berry-like, purple-black to almost black, about $1/4$ inch in diameter, edible; flesh juicy, purplish, containing 3-5 nutlets; maturing in late August. Bark gray-brown, warty, unpleasant odor if bruised. *Occurrence*: On rich open soils, thickets, stream banks, lowlands. *Similar species*: The red elderberry (*S. pubens*) has similar leaves except they are often lightly downy beneath. *Comments*: It is the fruit of this bush which provides us with the famous elderberry pies, jellies and wines.

RED ELDERBERRY HONEYSUCKLE FAMILY
Sambucus pubens *Caprifoliaceae*
Plate 28, Nos. 1 & 2

Description: Shrub 4-12 feet high, with widely spreading branches. Leaves compound, opposite, with 5-9 (usually 7) leaflets; individual leaflets lance-shaped, 3-5 inches long, edges finely toothed, tips sharp-pointed, dark green above, paler and often slightly downy beneath. Flowers bloom in late May or early June, in upright elongated cylindrical clusters; individual flowers dull yellow-white, tiny, with a strong odor. Fruit many in elongated clusters 3-5 inches long; individual fruit round, berry-like, bright scarlet, about $1/8$ inch in diameter, enclosing 3-5 nutlets, maturing in July. Bark gray-brown, warty. *Occurrence*: In shaded, rocky woodlands. *Similar species*: The blue elderberry (*S. canadensis*) has similar leaves, but it flowers and fruits much later in the year than the red-fruited species. The pith in broken branches is usually white. Pith in the red-fruiting species is usually brown. *Comments*: Despite its close relationship to the edible blue elderberry, the red fruit of this species is not edible.

WILD SNOWBERRY BUSH HONEYSUCKLE FAMILY
Symphoricarpos racemosus *Caprifoliaceae*
Plate 30, No. 3

Description: Shrub 1-4 feet high, with several stems and upright, slender branches. Leaves simple, opposite, 1-2½ inches long, oval, margins smooth, dull green above, paler beneath. Flowers bloom in August, in small terminal clusters; individual flowers bell-shaped, about ¼ inch long, white to pinkish white. Fruit a berry, borne in small clusters; individual fruit round to egg-shaped, snow white with a black spot at the tip, ¼-½ inch long; flesh white, enclosing 2 white seeds, maturing in September, sometimes persisting. Bark light brown to gray-brown, papery and shredding. *Occurrence*: In rocky, dry soils. *Similar species*: No other shrub fruits with large white berries. *Comments*: Snowberry is unique by having variable foliage. The leaves found on newer growth and younger shoots have large, coarse teeth. Also known as *S. albus*.

MAPLE-LEAVED VIBURNUM HONEYSUCKLE FAMILY
Viburnum acerifolium *Caprifoliaceae*
Plate 30, No. 4

Description: Shrub 3-5 feet tall, with ascending branches. Leaves simple, opposite, 3-5 inches long, maple-like, 3-lobed, coarsely and unevenly toothed, light green above, paler beneath. Flowers bloom in June in an upright cluster 2-3 inches across; individual flowers white, tubular with 5 spreading lobes, about ¼ inch across. Fruit several in an upright, flat-topped cluster 2½-3 inches across; individual fruit round with a nipple-like tip, flattened, about ¼ inch in diameter, nearly black, borne on a yellowish stem; flesh thin, dry, containing a single large stone, maturing in September. Bark smooth, gray to brown. *Occurrence*: In woodlands, especially on rocky soils. *Similar species*: Only the highbush cranberry (*V. trilobum*) has similar leaves, but it is a much larger bush with bright scarlet fruit. *Comments*: Has also been called maple-leaved arrow-wood and dockmackie.

HOBBLEBUSH
Viburnum alnifolium

HONEYSUCKLE FAMILY
Caprifoliaceae
Plate 32, No. 4

Description: A spreading shrub 3-9 feet high, with horizontal to drooping branches, often forming small thickets. Leaves simple, opposite, 4-8 inches long, broadly heart-shaped (like those of the basswood tree), finely toothed, light green above, paler and often downy beneath, turning red to purple in autumn. Flowers bloom in May, many in a flat-topped cluster 5-6 inches across; individual flowers of two types; marginal flowers sterile, white, tubular with five broad spreading lobes, almost 1 inch across; central flowers smaller, fertile, white, tubular with 5 small lobes. Fruit several in an upright flat-topped cluster 5-6 inches across; individual fruit oval, about ⅓ inch long, scarlet when young, turning deep purple when ripe, ripening unevenly so both colors appear in the same cluster; flesh dark, sweet, edible, enclosing a large flat stone, maturing in September. Bark smooth, dull purplish brown. *Occurrence*: In moist woodlands. *Similar species*: Only basswood has similar large, flat leaves, but these are alternately arranged on a large tree. *Comments*: Also called witch-hobble. Was *V. lantanoides*. Named for the way the low spreading branches obstruct and "hobble" the traveler. A pink flowering, later-blooming variety occurs in the Adirondacks.

Basswood Fruit
Tilia americana, page 110

WILD RAISIN HONEYSUCKLE FAMILY
Viburnum cassinoides *Caprifoliaceae*
Plate 32, No. 3

Description: Shrub 5-10 (sometimes 15) feet tall, with ascending branches. Leaves simple, opposite, 2-3 inches long, lance-shaped, margin usually smooth, tips pointed, deep green above, lighter beneath; stalk long, flattened, winged on both margins. Flowers bloom in mid-June, many in a rounded cluster 2-4 inches across; individual flowers white, 1/5 inch across, tubular with 5 spreading lobes. Fruit many in a cluster 2-4 inches across; individual fruit oval with a nipple-like tip, about 1/3 inch long, colors first yellow-green to pink to dark blue-black when mature, ripening unevenly so all color stages share the same cluster, borne on red stems; flesh dark, sweet, edible, enclosing a single flat stone, maturing in October. Bark brown-gray. *Occurrence*: In swamps and moist areas. *Similar species*: Nannyberry, (*V. lentago*) often grows nearby, but is a larger shrub with sharply toothed leaves and larger fruit. *Comments*: Also called withe-rod and Appalachian tea.

NANNYBERRY HONEYSUCKLE FAMILY
Viburnum lentago *Caprifoliaceae*
Plate 32, Nos. 1 & 2

Description: A shrub or small tree 10-20 (sometimes 30) feet tall, with many erect branches. Leaves simple, opposite, 2-4 inches long, oval to egg-shaped, finely and evenly toothed, tips pointed, deep green above, lighter beneath, turning red in autumn; stalk short, grooved with slightly winged margins. Flowers bloom in early June, in showy flat-topped clusters 3-5 inches across, tubular with 5 spreading lobes. Fruit many in a flat-topped cluster about 6 inches across; individual fruit about 1/2 inch long, oval with a nipple-like tip, almost black when ripe, borne on red stems; flesh dark, sweet, edible, enclosing a single flat stone, maturing in October, persisting. Bark reddish brown, becoming rough with age, with an unpleasant odor. *Occurrence*: In open woodlands, along streambanks and roadsides. *Similar species*: Wild raisin (*V. cassinoides*) often grows side by side with nannyberry. Wild raisin is a smaller shrub which blooms later (although some overlap occurs) and has smaller fruit. *Comments*: Also called sheepberry.

NORTHERN ARROW-WOOD
Viburnum recognitum

HONEYSUCKLE FAMILY
Caprifoliaceae

Plate 31, Nos. 1 & 2

Description: Shrub 5-10 (sometimes 15) feet tall, with many ascending branches; twigs ridged and usually smooth. Leaves simple, opposite, 1½-4 inches long, broadly egg-shaped, coarsely and sharply toothed, usually 10-20 teeth on each side, stalk short, dark green above, paler beneath, turning bronze red in autumn. Flowers bloom in late June, many on an upright flat-topped cluster 2-3 inches across; individual flowers white, tubular with five spreading lobes. Fruit several in an upright flat-topped cluster; individual fruit almost round, about ¼ inch in diameter, dark blue to bluish black; flesh thin, dry, containing a single large stone, ripening in September. Bark gray, smooth. *Occurrence*: On low and moist ground and in open fields. *Similar species*: No other *Viburnum* has such large, coarse teeth.

HIGHBUSH CRANBERRY
Viburnum trilobum

HONEYSUCKLE FAMILY
Caprifoliaceae

Plate 31, Nos. 3 & 4

Description: Shrub 4-14 feet high with ascending branches. Leaves simple, opposite, usually 3-lobed, maple-like, irregularly and sparingly toothed, lobe tips pointed, green above, paler beneath, turning red to purple in autumn. Flowers bloom in mid-June, in showy clusters 3-4 inches across; individual flowers of two types; marginal flowers sterile, white, tubular with 5 large spreading lobes, almost 1 inch across, central flowers smaller, fertile, white, tubular with 5 small lobes. Fruit many in usually drooping clusters 3-4 inches across; individual fruit oval, about ⅓-½ inch long, translucent scarlet; flesh juicy, edible but bitter and sour, enclosing a single saucer-shaped stone, ripening in October, often persisting through winter. Bark smooth, gray-brown. *Occurrence*: In open woodlands, in damp woods and along streams. *Similar species*: The European guelder rose (*V. opulus*) is a common ornamental escape. The two may be differentiated by the protruding glands found on the leafstem just below the blade. The tips of these glands are rounded and club-shaped in *V. trilobum* and concave in *V. opulus*.

BASSWOOD   BASSWOOD FAMILY
Tilia americana   *Tiliaceae*

Description: Tree 50-70 (occasionally 100) feet tall, with a single trunk unbranched ¼-⅓ of its height, the upper portions usually broad and rounded in outline. Leaves simple, alternate, 4-8 inches long, broadly heart-shaped with an uneven base, tips pointed, margins irregularly and sharply toothed, green above, slightly paler beneath, turning yellow in autumn. Flowers bloom in July, in small clusters suspended from the center of a narrow leaf-like bract; individual flowers greenish yellow to cream colored, pleasantly fragrant. Fruit forms in clusters like the flowers; individual fruit round, ¼-½ inch wide, dry, dull green, maturing in September, often persistent. Bark brownish gray, vertically fissured. *Occurrence*: Rich woodlands. *Similar species*: No other large tree has heart-shaped leaves or such unusually constructed flowers and fruit. *Comments*: The flowers make excellent honey. The fruit forms so rapidly following pollination that it is common to find both flowers and full-sized fruit on the same tree. At this young stage, the pea-like fruits may be boiled for an interesting, though rather bland, wild vegetable.

DAPHNE   MEZEREUM FAMILY
Daphne mezereum   *Thymelaeaceae*
Plate 33, No. 1

Description: Shrub 1-4 feet tall, with several erect stems and sparse foliage. Leaves simple, alternate, mostly clustered near branch tips, 3-4 inches long, lance-shaped, tips pointed, margins smooth, bright green above, paler beneath. Flowers bloom in May, before the leaves emerge, in groups of 2-5, each bloom springing directly from the stem; individual flowers about ½ inch long, tubular with 4 spreading lobes, lilac-like, rose, magenta or rarely white, with a very spicy fragrance. Fruit ¼ inch long, bright red, oblong, smooth-skinned, growing in clusters like the flowers, maturing in August and September. Bark light brown. *Occurrence*: Along streams and in damp wooded areas. *Similar species*: None. *Comments*: Introduced from Eurasia. It was named for the beautiful Greek nymph that was transformed into a laurel.

WINTERBERRY
Ilex verticillata

HOLLY FAMILY
Aquifoliaceae
Plate 33, No. 2

Description: Shrub or small tree 6-10 (sometimes 20) feet tall, with ascending branches. Leaves simple, alternate, 1½-3 inches long, oval to lance-shaped, tips pointed, sharp-toothed, dark green above, paler beneath, turning black in autumn, or sometimes falling with no color change. Flowers bloom in July, are greenish white, small and inconspicuous, in short-stalked clusters at the base of leafstems. Fruit borne in small clusters; individual fruit round, berry-like, brilliant red-orange, about ¼ inch in diameter; pulp yellow, not edible, typically enclosing 7 elongated yellow seeds; maturing in October, usually persisting until Christmas week. Bark smooth, dull, dark gray. *Occurrence*: In swamps and moist or low ground. *Similar species*: Smooth winterberry (*I. laevigata*) is a similar shrub that has narrower and more finely toothed leaves which turn yellow in autumn. It flowers and fruits earlier than the above species, and the long stemmed flowers and fruit occur only singly or in pairs. *Comments*: Also called black alder due to superficial similarities to the true alders, to which winterberry is not closely related.

SWEETGALE
Myrica gale

BAYBERRY FAMILY
Myricaceae
Plate 33, No. 3

Description: Shrub 2-5 feet high, with multiple stems and branches, often forming dense patches. Leaves simple, alternate, 1½-2½ inches long, paddle-shaped, broadest and toothed near the tip, dark green above, paler beneath, covered with minute golden resin dots, aromatic when crushed. Flowers bloom in May or June, in 1 inch catkins with triangular scales. Fruit cylindrical, woody, about 1 inch long, brown, made up of about 20 winged nutlets. Bark brown, cracked. *Occurrence*: In bogs and swamps and along lakeshores. *Similar species*: The barberry (*Berberis vulgaris*) has a similar leaf, but its stems are sharply thorned. *Comments*: A small and easily overlooked shrub.

MOUNTAIN HOLLY
Nemopanthus mucronata

HOLLY FAMILY
Aquifoliaceae
Plate 34, No. 1

Description: Shrub 3-10 feet high, with numerous ascending branches, trunk and branches slender. Leaves simple, alternate, 2-3 inches long, lance-shaped, margin mostly smooth with a few irregularly placed teeth, light green above, paler beneath. Flowers bloom in early June, usually solitary, borne on long slender stalks, from the base of leaves, minute, petals white and usually 4 (sometimes 3 or 5). Fruit berry-like, about $3/8$ inch in diameter, light red, dull, long-stemmed, enclosing 4-5 hard nutlets, maturing in August. Bark smooth, ash gray, irregularly marked with brown dots. *Occurrence*: Moist areas, stream banks and surrounding bogs. *Similar species*: Only certain honeysuckles also bear their flowers and fruit at the end of long stems, but the honeysuckles all have opposite leaves and much larger flowers. *Comments*: Mountain holly is the commonest member of the holly family found in our area, but its leaves have nothing in common with the famous holiday ornamental. Mountain holly leaves are pale, thin, not prickly and not evergreen.

SWEET-FERN
Comptonia peregrina

BAYBERRY FAMILY
Myricaceae
Plate 34, No. 2

Description: A low, branching shrub, 1-3 feet tall, sweet-scented, trunk thin, straight; branches ascending, spreading. Leaves simple, appearing alternate, 3-5 inches long, about $1/2$-$3/4$ inch wide, fern-like, margin deeply cut into regular lobes, dark green above, paler beneath, covered with tiny, yellow, resinous dots. Flowers bloom in May; male in short drooping catkins; female oval to round. Fruit a small burr surrounding small brown nutlets. Bark brownish, smooth. *Occurrence*: Prefers dry sandy soil. *Similar species*: At a distance, sweet-fern could be mistaken for a true fern, but no true fern develops leaves from a central, woody trunk. *Comments*: The aromatic fern-like leaves are spicy when dried and can be brewed into a pleasant tea. Formerly known as *Myrica asplenifolia*.

COMMON BARBERRY BARBERRY FAMILY
Berberis vulgaris *Berberidaceae*
Plate 34, No. 3

Description: Thorned shrub 3-10 feet tall, with many widely spreading and often drooping stems and branches. Leaves simple, alternate but clustered so to appear as rosettes, 1-3 inches long, oval to paddle-shaped, toothed along upper portion, bright green above, paler beneath, turning dull purple-green in fall. Flowers bloom in June, in showy drooping clusters 2-2½ inches long; individual flowers yellow, 6-petaled. Fruit a bright scarlet oblong berry, about ½ inch long, borne in drooping clusters; flesh juicy, pleasantly acid to taste, edible, enclosing 2 cylindrical, reddish brown seeds, maturing in October, persisting. Bark gray. *Occurrence*: Usually found in pastures and open woodlots. *Similar species*: Japanese barberry (*B. thunbergii*) is sometimes planted as a hedge border, and can escape. It is a smaller shrub with toothless, paddle-shaped leaves and rather dry flesh. *Comments*: An escape from Europe. Frequently attacked by farmers, because it is believed to be an alternate host for a species of wheat rust.

WITCH HAZEL WITCH HAZEL FAMILY
Hamamelis virginiana *Hamamelidaceae*
Plate 34, No. 4

Description: Small tree or shrub 5-20 (sometimes 25) feet tall, trunk short, bearing numerous spreading, crooked branches. Leaves 4-6 inches long, simple, alternate, oval, asymmetrical at the base, with wavy margins, dark green above, paler below, turning dull gold in autumn. Flowers showy, bright yellow, about 1 inch in diameter, occurring in small clusters directly attached to the twigs; petals four, long, narrow, usually curled and twisted; blooming in October and November. Fruit a brown woody capsule taking a full year to mature, splitting open in October to forcibly eject the 4 hard, brown seeds 15 or more feet away. Bark pale brown, mottled. *Occurrence*: Moist areas, along streams and wooded ridges. *Similar species*: None. *Comments*: Commercial witch hazel is distilled from the bark. The discovery of this extract is credited to an Oneida Indian.

COMMON BUCKTHORN
Rhamnus cathartica

BUCKTHORN FAMILY
Rhamnaceae
Plate 33, No. 4

Description: Shrub 5-12 feet tall, usually with a single main stem and ascending branches; branchlets tipped by a single sharp thorn. Leaves simple, opposite or almost opposite near branch tips, often alternate further back, 1½-2½ inches long, oval to almost round, tips pointed and often folded over, margins minutely toothed, waxy, green, becoming bronze yellow in autumn. Flowers bloom in June, in inconspicuous yellow-green clusters. Fruit occurs in small clusters at the base of leafstalks; individual fruit round, $3/8$ inch in diameter, purple-black; flesh juicy, purple, enclosing 4 dark purple seeds, maturing in September, persisting. Bark brownish gray. *Occurrence*: Young woodlots, hedgerows and moist areas. *Similar species*: Glossy-leaved buckthorn (*R. frangula*) has alternate leaves with smooth margins. *Comments*: The fruit of the buckthorn is purgative in nature and should not be consumed. Introduced from Europe.

GLOSSY-LEAVED BUCKTHORN
Rhamnus frangula

BUCKTHORN FAMILY
Rhamnaceae

Description: Shrub 5-12 feet tall, with a single main stem and stout ascending branches. Leaves simple, alternate, 1½-2½ inches long, oval to almost round, bluntly tipped, margin smooth, dark glossy green, becoming bronze yellow in autumn. Flowers bloom June through September, in small clusters; individual flowers greenish yellow, inconspicuous. Fruit occurs in small clusters, at the base of leafstalks; individual fruit round, $3/8$ inch in diameter, purple-black; flesh juicy, purple, enclosing 2-3 yellow and brown seeds, maturing in late August, persisting. Bark brownish gray. *Occurrence*: Young woodlots, hedgerows and moist areas. *Similar species*: Common buckthorn (*R. cathartica*) has toothed leaves. *Comments*: From July through September it is common to find this buckthorn displaying flowers, unripe fruit and mature fruit all at the same time. Introduced from Europe.

BUTTONBUSH   MADDER FAMILY
Cephalanthus occidentalis   *Rubiaceae*
Plate 35, No. 1

Description: Shrub 3-8 (sometimes 15) feet high, often with several crooked, ascending stems. Leaves 3-6 inches long, simple, opposite or whorled in threes or rarely fours, oblong to lance-shaped, tips pointed, edges smooth, dark green above, paler beneath, turning yellow in autumn. Flowers bloom in August, many crowded on a spherical head about 1 inch in diameter; individual flowers white, ⅓ inch long, tubular, thin, fragrant; the flower heads often in groups of three. Fruit small, dry, many crowded onto a spherical head about 1 inch in diameter, maturing in September and October. Bark brown-gray and smooth, darkening and cracking with age. *Occurrence*: In swamps and low moist ground, bordering slow moving or standing water. *Similar species*: The unique spherical flowering and fruiting head make misidentification with other species unlikely. *Comments*: Also called honey balls, in reference to the sweet fragrance of the flowers.

BLADDERNUT   BLADDERNUT FAMILY
Staphylea trifolia   *Staphyleaceae*
Plate 35, No. 2

Description: Shrub or small tree 6-15 (sometimes 25) feet tall, sometimes forming small thickets. Leaves compound, opposite, with three leaflets; leaflets 1½-2 inches long, oval, tips pointed, margins toothed, dark green above, paler beneath, turning yellow in autumn. Flowers bloom in early June, in drooping clusters; individual blossoms small, white, with 5 petals. Fruit an inflated pod, 2½-3 inches long, brown, 3-chambered, each chamber containing 1-4 (usually 1) small hard brown seeds, maturing in October, persisting into winter. Bark light gray. *Occurrence*: In rocky woods, hedgerows and riverbanks. *Similar species*: No other shrub has three-part leaves and large, inflated fruit pods. *Comments*: Also called rattle tree, for the noise made when the wind shakes the loose seeds around inside the pods.

AMERICAN SPIKENARD GINSENG FAMILY
Aralia racemosa Araliaceae
Plate 35, No. 4

Description: Shrub 3-5 feet tall, often with only a single main stem and two opposite spreading branches, very leafy in appearance. Leaves pinnately compound, 15-20 inches long, leaflets 15-21, broadly heart-shaped, tips pointed, margins sharply toothed, deep green. Flowers numerous, tiny, greenish white; in several rounded clusters along a central spike, blooming in late July. Fruit in clusters as described above; individual fruit round, small, reddish purple; flesh juicy, aromatic, enclosing 4-5 yellow kidney-shaped seeds, maturing in September. Bark smooth, very dark. *Occurrence*: Rich woodlands. *Similar species*: None. *Comments*: The large root was once used to make a spicy root beer.

BRISTLY SARSAPARILLA GINSENG FAMILY
Aralia hispida Araliaceae
Plate 35, No. 3

Description: Shrub 1-3 feet high, with a very prickly central stem. Leaves pinnately compound, alternate, 6-12 inches long; leaflets broadly lance-shaped, tips pointed, margins sharply toothed, green. Flowers bloom in early July, in several small rounded clusters at the plant's summit; individual flowers tiny, white, 5-petaled. Fruit occurs in clusters as described above; individual fruit about ¼ inch wide, round, purple-black; flesh juicy, enclosing 5 brown seeds, maturing in August. Bark smooth and reddish in the upper areas, heavily bristled, brownish and becoming woody near the base. *Occurrence*: Open sandy or rocky soils. *Similar species*: None. *Comments*: Was once called the wild elder. It is not related to our true elders (*Sambucus sp.*).

HOW TO MAKE A PRESSED LEAF COLLECTION

The study of trees and shrubs can be made more enjoyable by building a permanent collection of leaf samples from those species which you have identified. Preserving leaves is also useful in helping to later identify unknown species which you may encounter. In this case, comparison of your specimen to both the descriptions and the color plates found in this guide, combined with your own observation of whether the leaf grew in alternate or opposite patterns, should enable you to correctly identify your find.

To permanently preserve a leaf, begin by carefully picking it from the branch. Be careful not to damage the stipules at the stem's base. Remove any dirt, insects or moisture from the leaf surface. Place the leaf between the pages of a book with thick, absorbant pages, such as are found in old children's encyclopedias. Do not press leaves in books with a glossy finish on the pages. The leaves may stick to these pages and tear when you attempt to remove them.

If you plan to press several leaves within the same book, it is best to have at least ten pages between each specimen. Once your leaves have been placed in the book, close it and place a heavy weight, such as several more books, on it. Leave the weight on the book three to four weeks, by which time your leaf should be perfectly preserved. Since pressed leaves tend to curl and discolor if left out, it is best to permanently store them in an old book you pick for that purpose. You may wish to keep a card identifying the species with the leaf for future reference. Leaves pressed in this manner should last forever, giving you a permanent record of your plant studies.

GLOSSARY

Acorn	Fruiting body of an oak. A nut partially enclosed in a woody cap or cup.
Alternate	Growing spread out along a stem, but not opposite. See visual glossary.
Astringent	Tart to taste, puckery.
Assymetrical	Having two sides which do not match in size or shape. See visual glossary.
Base	The part of a leafblade that is closest to the stem. See visual glossary.
Blade	The wide, flat part of a leaf. See visual glossary.
Bloom	A white powdery coating found on many fruits, such as blueberries. Made up of yeast colonies.
Bract	A specialized leaf of different size and shape than the rest of the foliage, usually growing in association with flower or fruit clusters, as in basswood or American hornbeam.
Branch	The major growth off a central trunk. See visual glossary.
Branchlet	A smaller branch-like growth found along a true branch. See visual glossary.
Broad-leaf	Referring to any tree or shrub with flat leaves which are shed each autumn.
Bud	Structure containing young and unopened leaves or flowers. Usually covered with scales.
Burr	A heavily spined husk, containing one or several nuts.
Capsule	A dry and woody fruiting structure. It contains two or more chambers which split open at maturity, releasing numerous seeds.
Catkin	An elongated cluster of many small flowers or fruit, often slender, drooping and fuzzy.
Cone	Fruiting body of a conifer, made up of many closely overlapping scales enclosing the seeds.
Conifer	Literally means cone bearing. Leaves usually evergreen, such as in pine, fir, spruce or juniper.

Erect	Growing upright off a branch or branchlet.
Evergreen	A tree or shrub retaining most of the leaves through the winter.
Eye	A dark spot found at the tip of some fruit, made up of a dried remnant of the flower.
Flesh	The juicy part of a fruit, intended to nourish the seed.
Fruit	That part of a plant's reproductive system housing seeds capable of growing into new plants.
Herbaceous	A green plant that is not woody in the trunk or stalk, and dies back to ground level each winter.
Hip	The fruit of a rose. Usually spherical, brightly colored, with many seeds.
Husk	A tough coating found around some nuts, which may or may not split open at maturity.
Kernel	The fleshy part of a nut found within the shell, often edible.
Key	Fruiting body of ash, elm, and maple. They are single seeded, and attached to a flat wing. See visual glossary.
Leaflet	One of the three or more leaf-like parts of a compound leaf. See visual glossary.
Lobe	A large division of a leafblade, as in oak or maple. See visual glossary.
Margin	The edge of a leafblade. See visual glossary.
Nut	A hard one-seeded fruit with a thin to thick shell that does not split open upon maturity.
Nutlet	A small nut-like seed.
Opposite	Growing in pairs along a stem. See visual glossary.
Palmately compound	A compound leaf in which the leaflets spread out from the stem like fingers from a hand. See visual glossary.
Pendant	To hang down from a branch or branchlet.
Perennial	A plant that typically lives through three or more years.

Persisting	To continue remaining attached to a branch into winter or longer.
Petal	The broad leaf-like part of a flower, often brightly colored.
Pinnately compound	A compound leaf in which the leaflets are arranged along the stem in opposite pairs, except for the terminal leaflet. See visual glossary.
Pith	The center of a branch or stem, often spongy and soft.
Pod	A dry one-celled fruit that splits open at maturity. Each cell may contain one to several seeds.
Prickle	A sharp hair-like growth, used for protection. See visual glossary.
Scale	A small, flat and woody structure, usually somewhat rounded, that protects the seeds in cone or cone-like fruiting bodies.
Seed	The fertilized reproductive portion of a plant, capable of growing into a new plant.
Shrub	A woody-stemmed perennial green plant, not growing above 20 feet at maturity; often but not always with several main trunks.
Simple	A leaf with only one leafblade. See visual glossary.
Spine	A long, thin, woody, sharp growth, used for protection. See visual glossary.
Stem	The thin structure attaching a leafblade to a twig, not found in all plant species. See visual glossary.
Stipule	Small blade-like growths found at the base of the leafstem. Usually opposite and paired. See visual glossary.
Stone	A hard, bony structure, usually rounded, which appears to be a single unit but may actually contain more than one seed.
Teeth	Indentations along the margin of a leaf. See visual glossary.
Terminal	At the tip or end of a branch or stem.

Thorn	A short, sharp, woody growth, sometimes curved or hooked, used for protection. See visual glossary.
Tip	That part of a leaf or leaflet furthest from the base. See visual glossary.
Toxic	Poisonous.
Tree	A woody-stemmed perennial green plant, typically growing above 20 feet at maturity; often but not always with a single main trunk.
Trunk	The woody stem of a tree.
Twig	The smallest and newest growth off a branch or branchlet.
Whorled	Growing in a circular arrangement around a central stem, usually in multiples of three or four. See visual glossary.

Cassandra
Chamaedaphne calyculata, page 95

VISUAL GLOSSARY

TREE PARTS

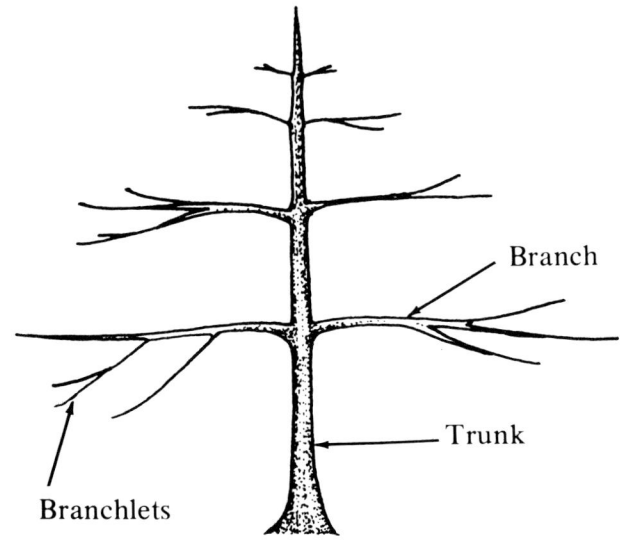

BRANCH ARRANGEMENT

Horizontal

Ascending

Spreading

PLANT ARMOUR

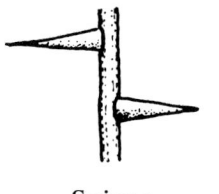
Spines

Thorns

Prickles

LEAF TYPES

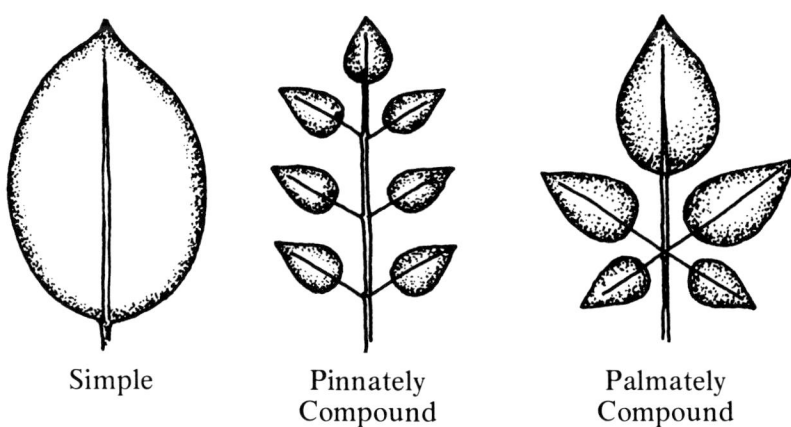

LEAF PARTS

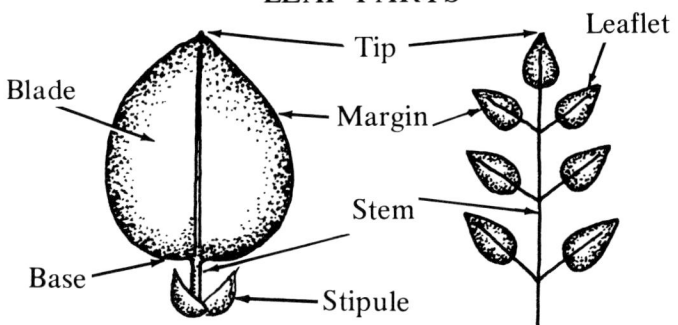

LEAF ARRANGEMENT

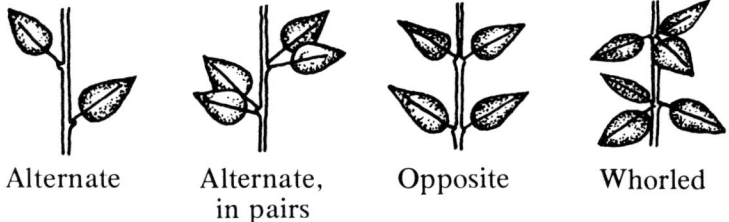

LEAF SHAPES

 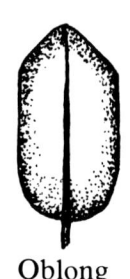 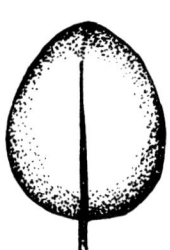  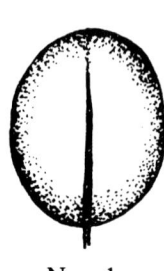

Oval   Oblong   Egg-shaped   Reverse egg-shaped   Nearly round

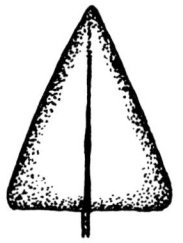  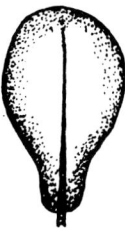 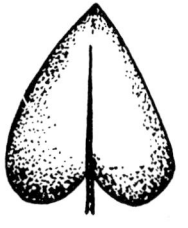 

Triangular   Lance-shaped   Paddle-shaped   Heart-shaped   Asymmetrical

LEAF TIPS

Rounded, blunt   Long tapered   Abruptly short-pointed   Notched

LEAF BASES

  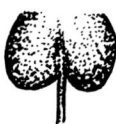

Rounded   Narrow, tapering   Heart-shaped

LEAF MARGINS

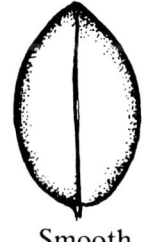
Smooth

Toothed

Lobed

TOOTHED MARGINS

Coarsely toothed

Finely toothed

Round or dull-toothed

Wave-toothed

Bristle-toothed

Double-toothed

CONIFER LEAVES

Needle-like

Blade-like

Egg-shaped overlapping

INDEX TO COMMON NAMES

Alder,
    Black   111
    European Black   30, **Pl. 8**
    Mountain   30
    Speckled   **30, Pl. 8**
Appalachian Tea   108
Apple   **47, Pl. 15**
Arbor Vitae   **20**, 21, **Pl. 3**
Arrow-wood,
    Maple-leaved   106
    Northern   **109, Pl. 31**
Ash,
    Black   102
    White   **102, Pl. 29**
Aspen,
    American   25
    Large-toothed   **25, Pl. 5**
    Quaking   25, 31
    Trembling   **25, Pl. 5**
Azalea,
    Apple   99, **Pl. 26**
    Wild   99, **Pl. 26**
Balsam Fir   **16, Pl. 1**
Barberry,
    Common   111, **113, Pl. 34**
    Japanese   113
Basswood   107, **110**
Bearberry   7
Beech,
    American   33, 34, **35, Pl. 10**
    Blue   33
    Water   33
    White   35
Beechnut   35
Bilberry   7
Birch,
    Black   30
    Gray   **31**, 32
    Ornamental White   31
    Paper   **31**, 101, **Pl. 8**
    White   31
    Yellow   **30, Pl. 8**
Bitternut   **28**
Blackberry,
    Common   **86, Pl. 19**
    Smooth   86
Black Locust   6
Bladdernut   **115, Pl. 35**
Blueberry,
    Dryland   100

Blueberry, *(continued)*
    Highbush   **100**
    Low   100
    sp.   100, 101
    Velvet-leaf   100, **Pl. 26**
Blue Colonel   **93**, 95, **Pl. 23**
Bog Rosemary   **96, Pl. 24**
Box Elder   6
Bristly Sarsaparilla   **116, Pl. 35**
Buckthorn,
    Common   **114, Pl. 33**
    Glossy-leaved   114
Butternut   **29, Pl. 7**
Buttonbush   **115, Pl. 35**
Cassandra   35, **95**
Cedar,
    Eastern Red   **21, Pl. 3**
    Northern White   20
    Swamp   20
Cherry,
    Black Choke   45, **Pl. 14**
    Choke   44, **45, Pl. 14**
    Eurasian Mazzard   44
    Fire   23, **44**
    Pin   44
    Rum   45, **Pl. 14**
    Sand   **44**, 47
Chestnut,
    American   **34, Pl. 10**
Chokeberry,
    Black   **48, Pl. 16**
    Red   **48, Pl. 16**
Cottonwood   **24, Pl. 5**
Crowberry   7
Currant   **40-41, Pl. 12**
Daphne   **110, Pl. 33**
Dewberry   7
Dockmackie   106
Dogwood,
    Gray-stemmed   **94, Pl. 23**
    Green Osier   **93, Pl. 23**
    Round-leaved   **94, Pl. 24**
    Red Osier   93, 94, **95, Pl. 24**
Elder,
    Wild   116
Elderberry,
    Blue   **105, Pl. 28**
    Red   **105, Pl. 28**
Elm,
    American   **39, Pl. 11**

Elm, *(continued)*		Kinnikinnik	93
Cork	39	Labrador Tea	**96, Pl. 24**
False	38	Lambkill	97
Slippery	**39, Pl. 12**	Larch,	
Water	39	American	20
White	39	Laurel,	
Fir,		Bog	97
Balsam	*See* Balsam Fir	Great	**98, Pl. 25**
Fly Honeysuckle	*See* Honeysuckle	Mountain	**98, Pl. 24**
Gooseberry	**40-41**	Pale	**97, Pl. 25**
Goosefoot	90	Sheep	**97, Pl. 25**
Grape	7	Maple,	
Guelder Rose,		Black	**92, Pl. 21**
European	109	Hard	92
Hackberry	**38, Pl. 12**	Mountain	**92, Pl. 20, Pl. 22**
Hardhack	**49, Pl. 17**	Norway	**92, Pl. 21, Pl. 22**
Hawthorn	**43,** 85, **Pl. 15**	Red	**91, Pl. 22**
Hazelnut,		River	91
American	**32, Pl. 9**	Rock	92
Beaked	**32, Pl. 9**	Silver	**91, Pl. 21, Pl. 22**
Hemlock,		Soft	91
Canadian or Eastern	16, **17,** 21, **Pl. 1**	Striped	**90,** 92, **Pl. 20, Pl. 22**
Ground	16	Sugar	**92, Pl. 21, Pl. 22**
Hickory,		Swamp	91
Bitternut	**28**	Water	91
Pignut	**28,** 29, **Pl. 7**	White	91
Shagbark	**29,** 36, **Pl. 7**	Meadowsweet,	
Highbush Cranberry	106, **109, Pl. 31**	Broad-leaved	**49, Pl. 16**
Hobblebush	**107, Pl. 32**	Narrow-leaved	**49, Pl. 16**
Honey Balls	115	Mountain Ash,	
Honeysuckle,		American	**46, Pl. 13**
Bush	**102,** 103, **Pl. 29**	Shrubby	**46, Pl. 13**
Common	**103,** 104, **Pl. 30**	Mountain Holly	**112, Pl. 34**
Early Fly	102, **103, Pl. 29**	Musclewood	33
Morrow's	103	Nannyberry	**108, Pl. 32**
Mountain Fly	**104**	Nettle-tree	38
sp.	99	Nine Bark	**85, Pl. 18**
Swamp Fly	**104**	Oak,	
Tartarian	103	Black	37, **Pl. 10**
Hophornbeam,		Burr	36
Eastern	**33, Pl. 9**	Chestnut	**36, Pl. 11**
Hornbeam,		Northern Red	**37, Pl. 10**
American	**33,** 35, **Pl. 9**	Swamp White	**36, Pl. 11**
Huckleberry,		White	**36, Pl. 11**
Black	**101, Pl. 27**	Oilnut	29
Ironwood	33	Pear,	
Juneberry,		Wild	**47, Pl. 15**
Bartram's	42	Pignut	**28,** 29, **Pl. 7**
Common	**42, Pl. 13**	Pine,	
Downy	42	Candlewood	18
Round-leaved	42	Northern Scrub	**17,** 18, 19, **Pl. 1**
Juniper,		Norway	18
Dwarf	**21, Pl. 3**	Pitch	**18, Pl. 2**
		Red	17, **18,** 19, **Pl. 2**

Pine, *(continued)*	
Scotch	17, 18, **19, Pl. 2**
Scots	19
Torch	18
White	**19, Pl. 2**
Plum,	
Canada	38, **43**
Wild	43
Poplar,	
Balsam	**24, Pl. 5**
Black	24
Lombardy	24
Necklace	24
Raspberry,	
Black	87
European Red	87
Purple-flowering	**85, Pl. 19**
Red	**87, Pl. 19**
Rattle Tree	115
Redbud	6
Rhodora	**99, Pl. 26**
Rose,	
Multiflora	**89, Pl. 17**
Pasture	**88, Pl. 17**
Prickly	**88, Pl. 18**
Smooth	88
Swamp	**89, Pl. 17**
Rosemary,	
Bog	*See* Bog Rosemary
Garden	96
Rowan Tree	46
Sarsaparilla,	
Bristly	*See* Bristly Sarsaparilla
Sassafras	6
Serviceberry	42
Shadberry	42
Sheepberry	108
Silky Colonel	93
Snowberry Bush,	
Wild	**106, Pl. 30**
Spicebush	6
Spikenard,	
American	**116, Pl. 35**
Spruce,	
Bog	22
Black	**22, Pl. 4**
Cat	22
Norway	17, 22, **Pl. 4**
Red	**22, Pl. 4**
Skunk	22
Swamp	22
White	**22, Pl. 4**
Steeplebush	49
Sugar-Berry	38
Sumac,	
Staghorn	**90, Pl. 20**
Sweetgale	**111, Pl. 33**
Sweet-Fern	**112, Pl. 34**
Sycamore	6
Tamarack	**20, Pl. 3**
Thimbleberry	85
Virginia Creeper	7
Walnut,	
Black	**29, Pl. 7**
White	29
Wild Raisin	**108, Pl. 32**
Willow,	
Bearberry	27
Black	**26**
Crack	**26, Pl. 6**
Goat	**27, Pl. 6**
Heart-leaved	27
Pussy	**27, Pl. 6**
Shining	27
Swamp	26
White	**26. Pl. 6**
Winterberry,	**111, Pl. 33**
Smooth	111
Witch Hazel	**113, Pl. 34**
Witch Hobble	107
Withe-Rod	108
Yew,	
American or Canadian	**16, Pl. 1**

INDEX TO BOTANICAL NAMES

Abies
  balsamea   11, **16, Pl. 1**
Acer
  dasycarpum   91
  nigrum   92, **Pl. 21**
  pensylvanicum   **90**, 92, **Pl. 20, Pl. 22**
  platanoides   92, **Pl. 21, Pl. 22**
  rubrum   **91, Pl. 22**
  saccharinum   **91, Pl. 21, Pl. 22**
  saccharum   **92, Pl. 21, Pl. 22**
  spicatum   **92, Pl. 20, Pl. 22**
Aceraceae   13, 90-92
Alnus
  crispa   30
  glutinosa   30, **Pl. 8**
  incana   30
  rugosa   **30, Pl. 8**
Amelanchier
  arborea   42
  bartramiana   42
  laevis   **42, Pl. 13**
  sanguinea   42
Anacardiaceae   14, 90
Andromeda
  glaucophylla   **96, Pl. 24**
Aquifoliaceae   112
Aralia
  hispida   **116, Pl. 35**
  racemosa   **116, Pl. 35**
Araliaceae   116
Aronia
  arbutifolia   **48, Pl. 16**
  melanocarpa   **48, Pl. 16**
  nigra   48
Berberidaceae   113
Berberis
  thunburgii   113
  vulgaris   111, **113, Pl. 34**
Betula
  alba var. *papyrifera*   31
  alleghaniensis   **30, Pl. 8**
  lenta   30
  lutea   30
  papyrifera   31
  papyrifera var. *cordifolia*   **Pl. 8**
  pendula   31
  populifolia   **31**
Betulaceae   12, 30-31
Caprifoliaceae   14, 102-109
Carpinus
  caroliniana   **33**, 35, **Pl. 9**

Carya
  cordiformis   **28**
  glabra   **28**, 29, **Pl. 7**
  ovata   28, **29, Pl. 7**
Castanea
  dentata   **34, Pl. 10**
Celtis
  occidentalis   **38, Pl. 12**
Cephalanthus
  occidentalis   **115, Pl. 35**
Chamaedaphne
  calyculata   35, **95**
Comptonia
  peregrina   **112, Pl. 34**
Cornaceae   13, 93-95
Cornus
  alternifolia   **93, Pl. 23**
  amomum ssp. *obliqua*   93
  circinata   94
  obliqua   **93**, 95, **Pl. 23**
  paniculata   94
  racemosa   **94, Pl. 23**
  rugosa   **94, Pl. 24**
  stolonifera   93, 94, **95, Pl. 24**
Corylus
  americana   32, **Pl. 9**
  cornuta   32, **Pl. 9**
  rostrata   32
Cupressaceae   20-21
Daphne
  mezereum   **110, Pl. 33**
Diervilla
  lonicera   **102**, 103, **Pl. 29**
Ericaceae   13, 95-101
Exobasidium
  rhododendri   **99, Pl. 26**
Fagaceae   12, 34-37
Fagus
  grandifolia   33, 34, **35, Pl. 10**
Fraxinus
  americana   **102, Pl. 29**
  nigra   102
Gaylussacia
  baccata   **101, Pl. 27**
  resinosa   101
Grossulariaceae   12, 40-41
Hamamelidaceae   113
Hamamelis
  virginiana   **113, Pl. 34**

Hicoria		*Populus*	
ovata	29	balsamifera	**24, Pl. 5**
Ilex		deltoides	**24, Pl. 5**
laevigata	111	grandidentata	**25, Pl. 5**
verticillata	**111, Pl. 33**	monilifera	24
Juglandaceae	13, 28-29	nigra	24
Juglans		tremuloides	**25, Pl. 5**
cinerea	**29, Pl. 7**	*Prunus*	
nigra	**29, Pl. 7**	americana	43
Juniperus		avium	44
communis	21	nigra	38, **43**
communis var. *depressa*	12, **21, Pl. 3**	pensylvanica	23, **44**
virginiana	11-12, **21, Pl. 3**	pumila	**44**, 47
Kalmia		serotina	**45, Pl. 14**
augustifolia	**97, Pl. 25**	virginiana	**45, Pl. 14**
latifolia	**98, Pl. 24**	virginiana	
polifolia	**97, Pl. 25**	var. *melanocarpa*	**45, Pl. 14**
Larix		*Pyrus*	
laricina	11, **20, Pl. 3**	americana	46
Ledum		communis	**47, Pl. 15**
groenlandicum	**96, Pl. 24**	malus	47
Lonicera		melanocarpa	48
bella	**103**, 104, **Pl. 30**	*Quercus*	
canadensis	102, **103, Pl. 29**	alba	**36, Pl. 11**
morrowii	103	bicolor	**36, Pl. 11**
oblongifolia	**104**	macrocarpa	36
sp.	99	prinus	**36, Pl. 11**
tartarica	103	rubra	**37, Pl. 10**
villosa	**104**	velutina	**37, Pl. 10**
Malus		*Rhamnaceae*	114
sylvestris	**47, Pl. 15**	*Rhamnus*	
Myrica		cathartica	**114, Pl. 33**
asplenifolia	112	frangula	114
gale	**111, Pl. 33**	*Rhododendron*	
Myricaceae	111-112	canadense	**99, Pl. 26**
Nemopanthus		maximum	**98, Pl. 25**
mucronata	**112, Pl. 34**	maximum X *canadense*	98
Oleaceae	14, 102	nudiflorum	99
Picea		roseum	**99, Pl. 26**
abies	12, 17, 22, **Pl. 4**	*Rhus*	
canadensis	22	typhina	**90, Pl. 20**
glauca	12, **22, Pl. 4**	*Ribes*	
mariana	12, **22, Pl. 4**	americanum	40-41
rubens	12, **22, Pl. 4**	cynosbati	40-41
Pinaceae	16-20, 22	glandulosum	40-41
Pinus		hirtellum	40-41
banksiana	11, **17**, 18, 19, **Pl. 1**	lucastre	40-41, **Pl. 12**
divaricata	17	nigrum	40-41
resinosa	11, 17, **18**, 19, **Pl. 2**	odoratum	40-41
rigida	11, **18, Pl. 2**	sativum	40-41
rubra	18	triste	40-41, **Pl. 12**
strobus	11, **19, Pl. 2**	*Rosa*	
sylvestris	11, 17, 18, **19, Pl. 2**	acicularis	**88, Pl. 18**
		blanda	88, 89

Rosa (continued)	
carolina	**88,** 89, **Pl. 17**
humilis	88
multiflora	**89, Pl. 17**
palustris	**89, Pl. 17**
Rosaceae	12-13, 42-49, 85-89
Rosmarinum	
officinalis	96
Rubiaceae	115
Rubus	
allegheniensis	**86, Pl. 19**
canadensis	86
ideaus	**87, Pl. 19**
occidentalis	87
odoratus	**85, Pl. 19**
strigosus	87
Salicaceae	12, 24-27
Salix	
alba	**26, Pl. 6**
caprea	**27, Pl. 6**
cordata	27
discolor	**27, Pl. 6**
fragilis	**26, Pl. 6**
lucida	27
nigra	**26**
uva-ursi	27
Sambucus	
canadensis	**105, Pl. 28**
pubens	**105, Pl. 28**
sp.	116
Sorbus	
americana	**46, Pl. 13**
aucupari	46
decora	**46, Pl. 13**
Spirea	
alba	**49, Pl. 16**
latifolia	**49, Pl. 16**
tomentosa	**49, Pl. 17**
Staphylea	
trifolia	**115, Pl. 35**
Staphyleaceae	115
Symphoricarpos	
alba	106
racemosus	**106, Pl. 30**
Taxaceae	16
Taxus	
canadensis	11, **16,** 21, **Pl. 1**
Thuja	
occidentalis	11, **20,** 21, **Pl. 3**
Thymelaeaceae	110
Tilia	
americana	107, **110**
Tiliaceae	110

Tsuga	
canadensis	11, 16, **17,** 21, **Pl. 1**
Ulmaceae	12, 38-39
Ulmus	
americana	38, **39, Pl. 11**
fulva	39
racemosa	39
rubra	**39, Pl. 12**
thomasii	39
Vaccinium	
angustifolium	100
corymbosum	**100**
myrtilloides	100, **Pl. 26**
pallidum	100
sp.	101
stamineum	**101, Pl. 27**
Viburnum	
acerifolium	**106, Pl. 30**
alnifolium	**107, Pl. 32**
cassinoides	**108, Pl. 32**
lantanoides	107
lentago	**108, Pl. 32**
opulus	109
recognitum	**109, Pl. 31**
trilobum	106, **109, Pl. 31**

ABOUT THE AUTHORS

Although William K. Chapman's education and professional experience is in the field of human services, his love of the outdoors dates back over three decades. Among those who have personally contributed to his knowledge of nature was the late Euell Gibbons. Mr. Chapman is frequently sought after as a speaker for many clubs, workshops and wild foods events. He has directed four wild foods festivals. He is currently coordinating an international project measuring time by means of natural floral clocks. He also teaches wild foods courses entitled, "Eating Out in Eden" at Utica College of Syracuse University. Mr. Chapman is the author of the wild food guide, *Hickory, Chickory and Dock*, author and illustrator of a ten year series of *Wild Foods Calendars*, and has written numerous articles on the study and research of wild plants.

Alan E. Bessette is professor of medical technology at Utica College of Syracuse University. He received a B.S. in medical technology from the University of Vermont, an M.S. in microbiology from the University of Oregon, and a Ph.D. in mycology from the University of Maine. His principle research interests include fungal and lichen morphology and taxonomy. Dr. Bessette is a naturalist for the Appalachian and Adirondack Mountain Clubs, advisor to the Mid York Mycological Society, and identification consultant for the New York State Poison Control Center. He has conducted numerous workshops and lectures on identification of edible and poisonous plants, identification and uses of lichens, and identification of edible and poisonous mushrooms. Dr. Bessette is the author of *A Guide to Some Common Edible and Poisonous Mushrooms of New York*, the Macmillan Field Guide: *Mushrooms—A Quick Reference Guide to Mushrooms of North America*, and *Mushrooms of the Adirondacks—A Field Guide*.

In preparing this book, we were not fortunate enough to locate any previous species list covering this vast area. We have made every effort to make this work as complete as possible. In the preparation of this book, we have been surprised both by the appearance of certain species and by the absence of others. If you are aware of any tree or shrub growing **wild** within the park but not found in this book, the authors would gratefully appreciate a note about the identity and location of such species. Address correspondence to:

William K. Chapman
P.O. Box 184
New Hartford, New York 13413

FIELD NOTES: